Praise for *The SI*

"*The SECRET SAUCE* is a great way for teachers and leaders to feel empowered to make meaningful change. Through conversational language that is filled with energy and passion, this book can help to make shifts needed in all schools. Let *The SECRET SAUCE* spill from its pages and fill your learning spaces with some amazing ideas."

—Dr. Robert Dillon, learner, leader, educator, coauthor of *The Space*

"Rich captures the practices, elements, and essence of what makes an effective educator. Instead of giving the 'Don't smile until Christmas' advice that Rich and I both received, give *The SECRET SAUCE!*"

—Evan A. Robb, principal, Johnson-Williams Middle School

"*The SECRET SAUCE* is the book for teachers who want to empower student voice and choice and build meaningful connections with students. This book is for any teacher, at any time in their career, who wants to create their own SECRET SAUCE and stir in just the right ingredients so learning will be delicious and never taste the same again."

—Barbara Bray, author, speaker, creative learning strategist, host of *Rethinking Learning* podcast

"*The SECRET SAUCE* combines wisdom with encouragement to cook up our own magic in order to make learning matter. Rich shares his adventures in the classroom, inspiring the reader to create a shared experience with students, honoring their ability to lead every step of the way. Full of practical ideas and reflections to make our own sauce, this book is one I certainly wish I had in my hands when I first began teaching."

—Nili Bartley, technology teacher, integration specialist, author of *Lead Beyond Your Title*

"Rich has compiled some of the most practical chapters I've ever enjoyed about being in education. The content is insightful, thoughtful, and brilliantly laid out to put you into meaningful action right away. *The SECRET SAUCE* cuts to the chase with its concise narrative, easy-to-digest summaries, and insightful reflection questions that will change the way you do your work for the better. This work is all about relationships, and Rich has laid out a game plan."

—**Houston Kraft**, cofounder of CharacterStrong

"Written from years of experience and from the heart, *The SECRET SAUCE* offers a guided reading experience for educators looking to focus on sound teaching and learning practices. Rich offers his recipe for designing and supporting classrooms that prioritize building connections to ideas and meaningful relationships."

—**Dr. Jennifer Williams**, educator and author

"Rich Czyz has written a practical guide for teachers on what it means to create a student-centered classroom. You too can find your own SECRET SAUCE—the combination of colleagues, influences, resources, strategies, and practical advice that will help you grow into an exceptional educator. As a teacher, you can empower your students to make meaningful change, and it starts with this book!"

—**Don Wettrick**, president, founder of the STARTedUP Foundation

"*The SECRET SAUCE* is chock-full of information about excellent practices in education that address the whole child. From ensuring that students are responsible for their own learning, to simplifying rules and time management, to restorative practices, Rich Czyz consolidates the critical 'must-dos' for his readers. *The SECRET SAUCE* makes for a delicious read!"

—**Pam Hernandez**, principal of Constable Elementary School, 2019 New Jersey Visionary Principal of the Year

"Rich Czyz is back with *The SECRET SAUCE!* This is a handy resource in which Rich shares his wisdom and expertise as an educator to inspire us to be the best we can be for our schools. This edu-culinary experience will provide teachers with a fresh approach to building student engagement in an engaging, sustainable way."

—**Sean Gaillard**, principal, author of *The Pepper Effect*

"*The SECRET SAUCE* by Rich Czyz is classic Rich. Mr. Czyz simply yet succinctly provides ingredients for educators to create a 'secret sauce' for success in the classroom. Rich begins his book discussing students and expectations and then stirs in culture, relationships, and other key herbs. He has provided the reader with the opportunity to plan and reflect after each chapter. This recipe is a keeper."

—**Mike Curran, Jr., EdD,** professor of
teacher education, Rider University

"I wish someone had handed me this book when I first started teaching! In *The SECRET SAUCE*, you will find the best-kept secrets for creating and customizing a recipe for success in your classroom."

—**Kasey Bell**, international speaker, blogger,
podcaster, author of *Shake Up Learning*

"Rich Czyz has written the book that new teachers and some seasoned teachers of today desperately need. He provides specific and practical ideas and strategies as support in the classroom and beyond. I foresee this book becoming the newest novice-teacher resource guide to be used during new staff orientations."

—**Dr. Josue Falaise**, director, Rutgers Institute for
Improving Student Achievement, Rutgers
University Graduate School of Education

"*The SECRET SAUCE* is a gift to new teachers, veteran teachers, and the profession of education. I'm disappointed that

I didn't have this book twenty years ago as a new teacher, but I'm thrilled to have it now. The *SECRET SAUCE* is pure awesome sauce."

—**Trevor Bryan**, arts educator, author
of *The Art of Comprehension*

"Great teachers just seem to know things that others don't. Well . . . the secret is out. Rich has figured it out, and he put it all down in this easy-to-read book. His combination of hard-earned wisdom and candid vulnerability make this a must-read for new and veteran teachers alike. I wish this book had been around when I started teaching."

—**Jon Harper**, assistant principal, author of *My Bad: 24 Educators Who Messed Up, Fessed Up, and Grew!*, host of *My Bad* and *Teachers Aid* podcasts

"Just as the finest chefs take great pride in using the best ingredients for their dishes, so has Rich crafted this amazing book of the very best strategies and ideas to help every teacher perfect their 'secret sauce' of instruction to engage students."

—**Marlena Gross-Taylor**, social commerce entrepreneur, founder of EduGladiators, author, speaker

"To be an exceptional educator, you have to be creative, inspired, and deeply human. In other words, embrace your special 'secret sauce.' This book is a guide for rewriting the classroom rules and rediscovering why you teach."

—**Tania Katan**, author of *Creative Trespassing*

"In his latest book, Rich crafts a powerful 'secret sauce' of creative insights, ideas, stories, and activities that will empower you as an educator and positively impact your students' learning. The book is thoughtfully designed around Rich's SECRET SAUCE acronym, giving readers a unique structure to begin implementing his creative approach, and most importantly, teaches you how to begin experimenting and creating your own."

—**Michael Cohen**, the Tech Rabbi, educator, speaker, author of *Educated by Design*

THE
SECRET SAUCE

Essential Ingredients for ~~Effective~~ *Exceptional* Teaching

RICH CZYZ

The SECRET SAUCE
© 2019 by Rich Czyz

> This book is available at special discounts when purchased in quantity for use as premiums, promotions, fundraisers, or for educational use. For inquiries and details, contact the publisher at books@daveburgessconsulting.com.

Published by Dave Burgess Consulting, Inc.
San Diego, CA
DaveBurgessConsulting.com

Cover Design by Genesis Kohler
Editing and Interior Design by My Writers' Connection

Library of Congress Control Number: 2019945766
Paperback ISBN: 978-1-949595-62-8
ebook ISBN: 978-1-949595-63-5

First Printing: September 2019

To all of the teachers and educators
who have inspired me
and challenged me
to be a better educator
through the years.

To all of those past and current educators
who have dedicated their lives
to improving the lives of their students.

To all of those who will enter
this noble profession to
make a difference for every student.
You won't be sorry.

Thank you.

Contents

Rules for Teaching

When I started teaching, my principal handed me a guide outlining all of my district's policies and a book laying out all of the procedural logistics to make me—supposedly—an effective teacher. The book had more than three hundred pages of instructions for the first few days of school, days certain to determine my success or failure for the remainder of the school year. If I simply put forth my best effort in those first few days, I would achieve a successful first year in the classroom. Or so I was led to believe.

Reading through the policy guide and instruction book felt overwhelming, at best. At worst, it simply rehashed the ground that had been covered in my education prep courses.

In hindsight, I realize that there are so many things about teaching no one ever told me. Certainly no one ever handed me the "secret sauce" of teaching.

I often wondered if such a "secret sauce" even existed. I frequently asked myself, *Will I ever be good at this? Or at least somewhat decent?* I struggled in the grandest sense of the word. On top of that, the advice and rules for teaching I was given were poorly stated and confusing:

- Don't smile until Christmas.
- Don't be a child's friend; they already have enough friends.
- Students who face the board learn more.

- Running an effective classroom is like running a restaurant: you need to manage students.
- Effective teachers don't make mistakes.

I had so many questions about these so-called "rules for teaching." Why wasn't I allowed to smile? Wouldn't this show the kids I liked them and was generally a pleasant person? Don't some students *need* a friend? What is so powerful about the board? No mistakes? A restaurant manager? I didn't know anything about managing a restaurant. These rules didn't help me at all!

It took me a long time to figure out how to be an effective teacher. In the process, I learned the hard way:

- I made mistake upon mistake before I figured something out.
- I learned from some great colleagues—and from some not-so-great ones.
- I attempted to watch, listen, and learn from other teachers as much as I could.
- I watched others make the same mistakes I did.
- I visited other classrooms and let colleagues visit my classroom.
- I accepted feedback from others, sometimes begrudgingly.
- I occasionally realized parents knew their children much better than I did.

With a great deal of patience and perseverance, and the occasional humble pie, I did all of these things, and I became a better educator. And guess what? Eventually I figured out a "secret sauce" to teaching did, in fact, exist. Now I'm passing it on to you in this book. Yes, it involves hard work. Yes, you will face peaks and valleys. Yes, you will struggle at times. You will be rewarded, however, by making a difference in the life of a child. Using the SECRET SAUCE can make you an *exceptional* educator.

What Exactly Is the SECRET SAUCE?

Student Voice/Choice

Expectations

Culture

Relationships

Errors

Time

Support

Authenticity

Utility in Design

Connections

Every Child (Every Day)

I've written *The SECRET SAUCE* because I want you to be a successful teacher, an effective teacher, an outstanding teacher! Actually, I want you to be more than successful, effective, and outstanding. I want you to use this SECRET SAUCE to become the *best* teacher you can be—a world-class educator who goes above and beyond to provide the most meaningful learning experiences for your students and to positively impact them every day.

The SECRET SAUCE is for each and every one of you, regardless of where you are in your career. You might be a brand-new teacher or only have been in the classroom for a very short time. Maybe you've just graduated from college and are looking for your first teaching job, or perhaps you've struggled through your first year in the classroom. *The SECRET SAUCE* can set you on the right path from the start, inspiring and laying the groundwork for meaningful connections with your students.

Perhaps you've been teaching for several years and are completely stuck in a rut. Maybe you've worked in the same assignment for a few years and know your content well but are not sure how to move forward. *The SECRET SAUCE* can provide some motivational tools to help you change the learning environment in your classroom.

Perhaps you're an experienced teacher who wants to reignite the spark—the reason you stepped into the classroom in the first place. Maybe you are near the end of your career, remembering the willingness you had to try new things to inspire your students when you started teaching. Over time, your daring spirit has waned, and you would give anything to rejuvenate your enthusiasm. *The SECRET SAUCE* can trigger that "new teacher" excitement again and make you feel as though you could spend twenty more years in the classroom.

It's time for all educators to move forward in their careers by bringing their best to the classroom, for themselves *and* their students. The secret doesn't need to be a secret any longer. No teacher needs to suffer in order to become a better educator and make a *greater* impact on students.

Find out what the SECRET SAUCE is all about. Read through the recipes. Mix in your own ingredients. Simmer. Stir. Taste. Adjust. Add some more seasoning. Turn up the heat. Invite another colleague to help make your unique sauce even better. It's time for you to be the head chef, choosing the right mix for your sauce to change the way your students approach learning. Make your own SECRET SAUCE and move forward with the knowledge that education and learning will never taste the same again!

Chapter 1

STUDENT VOICE AND CHOICE

The secret of education lies in respecting the pupil.

—Ralph Waldo Emerson

What You Need to Know: Allowing students to have a voice in their learning process by incorporating choice can empower students to take charge of their own learning and engage in personally meaningful and purposeful work.

My first formal observation came in late September during my rookie year as a teacher. As someone who was hired in late August, I only had a few weeks of teaching experience aside from student teaching. My math supervisor visited my classroom for a planned observation of a math lesson with my fifth-grade students, and I was sure my game of "math baseball" was going to impress him. Students were split into two teams, and each team sent one player to the board to solve a problem while all the other students sat and watched. I even had bases placed around the classroom. If a student answered a question correctly, he or she used a spinner to try for a single, double, triple, or home run. If a student answered the question incorrectly, he or she received an "out" for their team.

While I was very nervous before the observation began, somehow I managed to make it through the forty-five-minute lesson with only minor hiccups. After the lesson, my supervisor left without providing any real feedback. I felt good about the lesson but not great, and I waited in anticipation for the written observation to appear in my mailbox. When it finally arrived a few days later, I opened the envelope with trepidation. After I read the first few lines of the report, I realized the lesson had not gone as well as I had thought. While my supervisor had been highly critical of the lesson and not me as a teacher, I couldn't separate the two.

As I sat at my desk, completely devastated and reading the entire observation report a second and third time, I had to agree with everything it said. Of course calling students to the board one at a time to solve a problem—while the other twenty-six sat aimlessly—was a *huge* problem! While I intended for my lesson to be motivational, I missed the entire objective: for all students to practice three-digit addition and subtraction. I sat there stunned. I didn't know what to do; I didn't know how to recover. My supervisor did not pull any punches when delivering feedback, and in that moment, I felt like the worst teacher in the world, with no hope of ever coming back from this setback.

As I look back, I realize this was one of the greatest learning experiences of my career. This supervisor eventually became my principal and mentor as I completed my administrative coursework. Years later, when I reminded him of the observation, he laughed about how overcritical he had been. Even so, I always tried to remember what he taught me: all children should be able to contribute his or her voice to every lesson!

One Question, One Answer

One question. One student called upon. One answer. Repeat.

I have seen this done in so many classrooms with so many students completely disengaged. They may know the answer or have a great contribution to make in a discussion, but instead, they sit passively, don't participate, and watch the same students answer simple questions with one predetermined answer over and over again.

One thing you can immediately take away from this book is learning to replace "one question, one answer" with "many questions, many answers." In an engaged classroom, there will be follow-up questions, student questions, student answers, rebuttal, agreements, disagreements, more questions, discussions, conversations, and a whole lot of thinking.

Try these simple strategies to change up your questioning routine:

Everyone shares for every answer. Any time you ask a question, let every student share an answer. This can be accomplished through a simple "Pair-Share." After asking a question, let each student turn to a partner and share his or her thoughts as you walk around the room and listen to answers. You won't get to hear every answer, but sometimes you'll hear some magical conversations among kids who normally wouldn't share with the large group because sharing with one person is less stressful and risky. At this point, ask the students if they want to share with the entire group, or if they are uncomfortable contributing aloud, offer to share what you heard for them.

The power of the follow-up question. When you ask one question, receive one answer, and move on, you miss the opportunity for critical thinking and discussion. Pair your basic fact-based questions with powerful follow-up questions, such as the examples below:

- Why? Can you provide evidence for your answer?
- How did you reach or find your answer?
- Do you agree or disagree with your fellow student's answer? Why?
- Share three reasons for giving your answer with the person next to you.

What? So what? Now what? By using this simple set of questions, you can go beyond fact-based responses. *What?* asks for simple information. *So what?* asks students to interpret the information. *Now what?* asks students to apply the information to a given situation or to a more personalized context. You can utilize this follow-up structure across your curriculum, giving students the opportunity to engage in deep analysis and application of skills and content.

Question flooding. One of the best ways to encourage students to ask quality questions is to give them the opportunity to practice coming up with their own questions. Throw out a concept or topic and ask students to generate as many questions as they can about the subject. No question is off-limits. Students just come up with questions and write them down. Once students have their lists of questions, ask them to combine or revise questions to avoid overlap and narrow down the list to begin their own research on the topic.

Meant to Be Heard

For many years, educators have focused on getting students to comply. They use hand signals to quiet students quickly, or ask students to raise their hands before speaking—as if anyone in the real world does this when sitting at the dinner table! (My children actually have done it, but I quickly reminded them they *don't* need to raise their hands to speak!) Educators often admonish the student who has too much to say—or worse yet, complain about the child to other teachers in the faculty room. Some educators even use the phrase, "When the hand goes up, the mouth goes shut" in an effort to silence students.

Sadly, educators have always seemed very impressed and *surprised* when a child says something intelligent, although they rarely give them the opportunity to do so. In an effort to gain full compliance from students, some variation of "be quiet" has dominated our schools for far too long. In fact, many of these tactics are still used in schools today, forcing students to be voiceless. After all, children are "meant to be seen and not heard," right? Wrong!

This is one of the biggest problems in schools today. Students have something to say, but they are being shut down. Many students go through an entire school day without sharing their voices in meaningful ways. They sit quietly, waiting for someone to engage them, only to realize no adult is interested in hearing what they have to say. When adults don't take the time and put forth the effort to hear each student's voice, they have wasted the most important and valuable resource in the world.

So how do you engage students in relevant and purposeful discussions? How do you empower each one of them to speak out? What do you do for the quiet student who sits in the back of the classroom and barely contributes his or her voice? How do you help that student tell the world his or her story? Every student *does* have a story, and it needs to be shared.

For me, Fiona was that student. She was one of my fifth-grade students, and she had quite a story to tell; however, almost an entire year passed without it being told. A few months into the school year, Fiona had barely uttered a single word. My co-teacher and I had expected this since the fourth-grade team had briefed us about her being a very quiet girl who rarely contributed to the conversation. She lived up to the description, though my colleague and I certainly attempted to engage her in conversation. My effort to develop a relationship with Fiona seemed almost like a game to her. When I tried to talk to her, she gave the slightest smile but did not utter a single word. I wasn't sure if she lacked confidence or if she just didn't like me. My co-teacher was luckier. She at least conjured one-word answers from Fiona. In fact, this was the only reason I knew what Fiona's voice sounded like.

By the time parent-teacher conferences rolled around in November, we were getting nowhere. That is, until Fiona's mom let an important fact about Fiona slip as our meeting ended. She told us Fiona would be missing a couple of days of school because she was getting ready to present her show dog at a competition. I sat there almost too stunned to ask a follow-up question, but I'm glad I did. "Did you say Fiona is going to show her dog at a competition?" I asked.

It turned out that Fiona was actually a very accomplished dog handler and was preparing for a junior kennel club show. While she wouldn't say a word to me at school, she got up in front of many adults at dog shows each week, trotted along with her dog, and showed off its skills. More importantly, she demonstrated her own skills and confidence. I was completely stunned, but it gave me a way in.

From that moment on, my relationship with Fiona changed. I was fascinated by her role as a dog handler, especially at her age, and I asked her questions about it. She suddenly had a reason to share her voice with me and the class, and eventually, she did just that. It was one of the most magical moments of the school year. It is rare that students are accomplished dog handlers and, unfortunately, very few students have the opportunity to share their passions with their classmates and teachers. I am fortunate to have learned of Fiona's passion and didn't waste the opportunity to encourage her to share it.

Giving Students Voice and Choice

Giving students *voice* and *choice* in their own learning does not need to be complicated. It can actually be rather easy to implement aspects of *choice* within your classroom to encourage students to share their *voices*. Try these simple strategies for giving students a say in their own learning:

Give students ownership over classroom routines and procedures. Let them figure out together what flow works for them, instead of choosing one solely to make your life easier. You never know, students may come up with a better workflow for themselves, their classmates, *and* their teacher than you might have. Give students a choice in how they approach their work in the classroom, and they will take ownership over the learning routines and options:

- Let students work together to set up furniture in a way that helps them learn most efficiently and effectively.
- Let students decide where to keep materials in the classroom. Does it make more sense to let students keep their own crayons at their desks, or should there be a communal basket of crayons? Depending on the students, the two options may need to coexist.
- Let them decide whether they work best with a pencil, pen, marker, Smencil—a "Smelly (scented) Pencil" for those who have not been initiated yet—or another writing utensil. Some will prefer to work with erasable pens; some might like Sharpies. (I prefer the combo Sharpie pen in blue, in case you're thinking about my birthday gift.) A student might use the "World's Smallest #2 Pencil," having sharpened it down to only a quarter inch of wood between the point and the eraser. As long as students feel comfortable, what they write with doesn't matter.

Allow students choice in how they demonstrate learning. Not every student does well when forced to take an end-of-chapter or end-of-unit test. If you haven't noticed this yet, just take a look at the stress levels of some of your students before their next scheduled test. There are many ways in which students can choose to demonstrate learning in the classroom:

- Let them create a visual representation of what they learned in any given lesson. They could make a sketchnote showing what they learned about the water cycle and its impact on the environment. Maybe another student will want to record a video showing real-life examples of the water cycle in action.
- Take advantage of student strengths when designing assessment options. If a student is an excellent singer or a gifted lyricist, let him or her write a song about life through the eyes of Jonas from *The Giver*. Does a student really love to cook and want to become a future chef? Let him or her prepare a meal for classmates demonstrating the dining behaviors of a particular culture.

Let students choose whether to work collaboratively or independently. Assessing students through a group project seems like a great idea until you realize one student in the group did ninety percent of the work. One member of the group was happy to shirk responsibilities for the day, and the other two members are angry because the final product didn't represent their knowledge of the content. Sometimes students may want—or even *need*—to work by themselves to best demonstrate what they have learned.

Use student surveys to find out what's working and not working in your classroom or school. If you want to know if your school is succeeding in its educational goals, you should ask the opinions of those who matter most—the students. A simple survey about important school factors like culture, climate, operations, and instruction given to students can provide helpful information to improve the school:

- Ask students to complete a survey at the end of the year reflecting on the instructional strategies, activities, and experiences they encountered throughout the year. Which experiences held the most meaning? Which activities could they have lived without?
- Start a lesson by asking students to select one of three articles to read about a content topic. Find a student volunteer to lead each group in discussion about their chosen articles as you walk around to monitor and support.
- If student behaviors are negatively impacting the classroom as soon as students finish an activity or assignment, give students a survey to find out what projects or endeavors they would like to participate in when they finish. Give them options, such as reading books, drawing and coloring, Genius Hour, or critical thinking games like Connect 4 or Disruptus. Students may even suggest something you hadn't thought of to keep them positively engaged.

As educators, we know *choice* can motivate students to learn. When students get to select their materials or resources, or determine how they are assessed, they are much more likely to engage in meaningful, memorable learning. Incorporate *choice* to encourage student *voice* as much as you can. Give students a reason to take ownership of their learning experience and let them speak for themselves. It is said that the person doing the most talking is often doing the most learning. Give your students a *voice* in *what* they learn, *when* they learn, *where* they learn, and *how* they learn. When you do this, you will automatically help students to be more invested in *why* they learn.

The Power of Yes

Sometimes a student will come to you with an idea. It could be simple and easy to execute, like, "Hey, Mr. Czyz, can we read *Mr. Popper's Penguins* as a class this afternoon?" But it might also be completely outlandish and difficult to implement, like, "Hey, Mr. Czyz, can we build a playground in the gym so we have somewhere to play during indoor recess?"

When this student brings you his or her idea, whether it is big or small, you can respond in three ways:

- No
- Maybe
- Yes

If you respond with *No*, you are essentially saying to the student, *No. Your idea is terrible, and I'm not interested in trying to figure out the logistics involved in implementing it.* Even if you don't *say* the second part, the student hears it in his or her mind.

If you begin your response with *Maybe*, you are basically telling the student, *Maybe. I don't want to say yes, but I also don't want to say no because I want to spare your feelings. If you continue to ask me, though, the eventual answer will probably be no.* Here your response shows lukewarm interest in anything the student cares enough about to ask about.

If you start your response with *Yes,* you are demonstrating that you care about the student's idea. *Yes. Absolutely! What a great idea! I care so much about you and your idea that we will do whatever it takes to make it a reality. If we can't, though, we will find something else that honors your original idea.*

If you were a student, which of those responses would you want to hear? Remember, *yes* can have a powerful positive effect, while *no* can completely derail your relationship with a student even before it begins. *No* can limit a student before they even get started. It places limitations and creates a negative culture around asking questions and sharing ideas in the classroom. Try answering with *Yes, if...* Such a response makes the impossible possible. It encourages curiosity, creativity, and confidence. When students face a thousand *No*'s on a regular basis, a single *yes* can make all the difference. Say *yes* as often as you can!

When students face a thousand No's on a regular basis, a single yes can make all the difference. Say yes as often as you can!

SECRET SAUCE SUMMARY

- Stop asking one question and calling on one student for one answer. Give every student a chance to answer every question. Use a Pair-Share or other discussion strategy, or have each student jot his or her answer on a sticky note.

- Focus less on compliance and getting students to "be quiet." Develop a reasonable way to incorporate all student voices—even the shy, quiet ones—throughout the day.

- Get to know students. Learn their likes and dislikes. Ask questions about the things they are most passionate about.

- Stop saying *no* to students. Live by the *Yes, if...* philosophy. Do everything possible to accommodate student interests and requests. Explain the conditions needed to allow students to move forward with the projects and experiences they find most meaningful.

- Incorporate as much *choice* as possible into classroom routines and procedures, assessments, projects, and passion-based learning. Use surveys to find out what's working and not working for students.

Planning and Reflecting

In what ways do you currently provide *choice* to students? How can you give students more opportunities to choose within your daily lessons?

_____

_____

_____

How do you encourage the "voiceless"—the students who don't normally contribute or share aloud—to participate? What strategies do you employ to ensure every student can share during a lesson?

_____

_____

_____

When was the last time you said *no* to a student? Why did you say *no*? Under what conditions could you have said *yes*?

_____

_____

_____

What can you do to motivate all students to share their *voices* when given the opportunity?

_____

_____

_____

Add Your Own SECRET SAUCE Ingredients

List three actions you will take to give students more *choice* within your lessons.

1. _____

_____

_____

2. _____

_____

_____

3. _____

_____

_____

Chapter 2
EXPECTATIONS

Whether you think you can, or you think you can't—you're right.

—HENRY FORD

What You Need to Know: Establishing high expectations is necessary for students, and absolutely necessary to run a successful classroom, but those expectations *must* be accompanied by enough support to help students meet them.

---

once had a colleague whose two favorite words were *can't* and *won't*.

My students can't do that.

My students won't be able to do that.

She was a constant chorus of negativity. As an adult, I found it hard to listen to her talk about what her students couldn't or wouldn't do. For her students—who often heard those words, along with a lot of *no*'s thrown in for good measure—it had to be an awful experience. On several occasions, I tried to intervene.

Have you ever tried— I would start to ask. But her surly response cut me off before I could finish my question. *You don't know my students.*

She always had a response, always a reason why her students *couldn't.* She firmly believed her students were incapable of success, and because of her expectations, she was right. She always reminded me of the Henry Ford quote noted above.

Actually, even *I* was afraid my colleague was right. Her students would not succeed while they were with her. They could not and would not because she set the bar so low. Student performance suffered because of her unrealistic expectations. The only way I could show she was wrong was to prove that one of her students *could be* successful.

Enter Nick. Nick was a student who struggled academically because of a specific learning disability. He also struggled because he was constantly being told he *couldn't.*

Nick, you can't do that. It's too hard for you.

No, Nick. You won't be able to do that. Why don't you try something easier?

When students are persistently told they can't be successful, they begin to believe it. Nick needed to be successful at *something*—so he became successful at disrupting the class. He avoided work by sharing jokes out loud with the whole group. Nick and the teacher were constantly arguing about what he was supposed to do when he wouldn't—or couldn't—complete his work. Additionally, he sometimes took his jokes with classmates too far, and there were consistent problems with Nick fighting with classmates as a result. Every day was a struggle for Nick because he was always told he couldn't be successful. Worst of all, my colleague shared her opinion of Nick with everyone. In the faculty room, she continually talked about what a "problem" Nick was and how no one could ever reach him.

As I said, I tried to suggest that students could be academically successful if she just took a different approach. I'm not sure why she didn't think that her students could experience greater success. I knew it was likely something outside her control that may have happened in her educational career to make her feel this way. I had no idea what it was, but my colleagues and I weren't getting through to her. I wish she found her SECRET SAUCE so Nick's education could have been more effective.

Consequences and Rewards
by Trevor Bryan

Consequences

If you do not do your work...

- I will sit with you;
- I will talk with you;
- I will listen to you;
- we will work together to figure out a plan so you can do your work;
- I will support you so you can be successful; and
- I will root for you, no matter what.

Rewards

If you do your work...

- your voice will be heard;
- your ideas will be shared;
- your uniqueness will be celebrated;
- your dreams will be built;
- I will support you so you can be successful; and
- I will root for you, no matter what.

My co-teacher and I learned in late May that Nick would be joining us for fifth grade before moving on to middle school. We knew this was the perfect opportunity to show what he was capable of if he was encouraged to be successful and supported in those expectations. We knew if we didn't try something different, he would continue to struggle, and we would continue to struggle with him all year long. We couldn't let that happen.

On "Meet Your Teacher Day" in late August, Nick and his mom entered our classroom. We told Nick how excited we were for him to join our class and how we thought he would have a very successful year. I'm sure they seemed like empty words to Nick at the time, especially after his previous experience. Starting on the first day of school, however, we began to prove we had meant it. We constantly helped Nick understand what the expectations were. We wouldn't constantly battle with Nick about his work because we told him exactly what work he needed to complete and supported him in completing it. Fights between Nick and his classmates wouldn't occur because we showed him how making jokes could be fine when appropriate, but it was never okay to make a joke at someone's expense. We modeled this for Nick and his classmates and supported him when he made a mistake.

I'd like to say Nick turned around quickly, but he didn't. He struggled at times, but we kept reinforcing our expectations and provided support every step of the way. Fifth grade turned out to be Nick's most successful year ever. He even reached second honor roll by earning a combination of As and Bs during the last marking period.

The expectations *and* support—more on this later!—made all the difference for Nick. We started with the belief that all students *can* and *will be* successful. Every student has the ability to learn. Some will need more help than others, but it is extremely important to let each student know he or she is expected to learn.

Unfortunately, when expectations are low, students will sink to meet them. When held to higher expectations, many students will rise to achieve them. Think for a moment about the teachers you know who have low expectations about how students can or can't learn. In some cases, students may have learned, simply to spite these teachers, but in most cases, low expectations probably led to minimal achievement. Establishing your expectations for students is key to successfully meeting your students' needs.

How can you hold students to higher expectations? Start by working directly with students and providing strong support—more on this in chapter seven—to ensure students are able and confident enough to meet expectations.

A teacher with high expectations does the following:

- believes all students can *and* will learn when they engage in their passions;
- makes expectations clear so all students know exactly what they need to do; and
- works with students to develop goals aligning with class expectations.

A teacher who provides strong support does the following:

- believes all students should be allowed to meet expectations at their own paces, understanding that some children may require more or less time;
- assures students that he or she will be beside them at every step as students work toward goals;
- offers modifications and makes accommodations to help each student achieve success; and
- models the actions associated with his or her expectations so students understand how meeting expectations looks, sounds, and feels.

Expectations versus Rules

For some teachers, *expectations* become synonymous with *rules* and are only reviewed for the first couple of days of the school year. The "class expectations" are then written on a fancy poster, hung on the wall, and never referred to again until someone breaks one of those "rules." Expectations, however, should never be confined to one class period or one week of school or to a poster. Expectations need to be a living and breathing part of your classroom—almost like a twenty-sixth student. Every child deserves to know what to expect every day, and teachers must constantly live and model those expectations. You can set your expectations for students on the first day of school, but you must go well beyond that. The first day of school receives all the fanfare and glory, but it is not when the real work is done. The excitement of new clothes and new faces gives way to the serious matter of building a community of learners. The second day and beyond is when teachers need to get down to what really matters: modeling expectations and continuously showing students how to learn on their own.

If you expect students to internalize your rules for the classroom in a single class period and immediately move to content work, you have set the bar for every day to follow. You will invariably struggle to motivate students. Their focus will be on compliance, and you will join the constant chorus of *no!* Students will know exactly what to expect: *I have to sit in my seat, do exactly what I'm told, and not go beyond that.*

They will ask things like, "I'm done. What should I do now?" or say things like, "Mr. Czyz, you didn't tell me I needed to do it that way." Every detail needs to be laid out step by step so that students can complete "paint by numbers" activities. They are once again a part of the performance of "playing school." You can expect them to do exactly what they were asked to do and nothing more or less. This is the definition of compliance we need to avoid in our classrooms.

The Poster in Your Room

You may want to hang the "rules" poster in your classroom; it certainly makes referring to it easy. You may have seen others share their expectations in a list of things students can and cannot do.

Resist the urge to do this.

Instead, consider something I saw once when I walked into a second-grade classroom during the first week of school. Students were about to engage in their first teamwork challenge of the year: trying to stack cups without using their hands.

This poster hung on the wall:

As I walked in, the teacher was explaining the rules for the teamwork challenge, and I heard, "Each team needs to work together."

I was most impressed when a seven-year-old girl added to the rules by saying, "It doesn't matter how long we take to do it. It doesn't matter who finishes first."

The teacher responded, "That's right. It's important to be a learner, not a finisher."

The poster had only been hanging in the room for five days, and already the student had started to internalize it.

A poster can exist as a constant part of the classroom, almost like another student who participates each day. But the poster should establish *expectations* in the classroom, not limitations. Don't let the poster simply provide a list of things to do or *not* do.

Most of all, make sure the students and teachers in the room are living the words each day.

Be a learner, not a finisher.

Setting Expectations

How can you set high expectations for performance and participation in your classroom? Try the following strategies for defining your expectations with students:

Go simple! Many teachers start the year by providing students with a list of rules. The list is usually extensive and might include several items with a negative tone: no talking, no chewing gum, no cell phones, etcetera. In some cases, a more positive connotation may be used: come to class on time, listen and follow directions, be respectful of others, etcetera. Either way, the list is long and can be cumbersome and limiting when it comes to holding students to high expectations. Sometimes students need something different from the prescribed consequence. Keeping a few simple rules allows flexibility and the ability to be fair, though not necessarily equal. All students should get exactly what they need, and they should understand this through a simple set of rules. Try something like this: *Respect yourself, respect others, and respect the classroom.* Almost everything related to discipline and students not meeting expectations is covered in phrases like this.

Set goals with students. Start by asking students what they would like to accomplish during their time with you. When you have an idea of what goals students are working toward, you can establish your expectations more easily. This is also especially helpful in determining what sort of support your students need to be successful. If an individual student in your classroom is working toward writing his own comic book, for example, you will need to hold him or her to high expectations as a writer and creator. You will also need to provide support in the form of comic book exemplars—maybe a mentor well versed in drawing and a group of peers willing to provide meaningful feedback would be helpful. Knowing what drives your students can help you mold and modify your expectations to better fit their needs.

Start with questions. When you are establishing expectations in the classroom, begin with questions that can guide discussion and provide insight into students' understanding of what's expected of them. Consider the following questions as you make your own list:

- What do you expect from one another?
- How should you treat one another?
- What do you expect from the teacher?
- What should the teacher expect from you?
- What happens when someone is not meeting the shared expectations?

- What does it mean to "own" your learning?
- How can you best complete your work?
- What happens if you struggle?
- How do you get help from the teacher?

While this list is not exhaustive, asking these questions will help you determine students' priorities. You can learn a lot about how much support individual students may need when you hear them honestly discussing and attempting to answer these questions. You will learn exactly how much modeling they need. While most students know not to run in the school hallway because it is not safe, for example, the true test comes when we find out if all students are able to meet the expectation of walking safely in the hallway.

SECRET SAUCE SUMMARY

- Students must know high expectations exist within the classroom and must feel supported to meet them.

- Resist the urge to boil classroom expectations down to a list of dos and don'ts on a classroom poster. Expectations need to be a living part of your classroom and modeled at all times.

- Work with students to develop classroom expectations. Start with simple expectations for how students should treat peers, teachers, and other staff members.

- Help students set goals related to classroom expectations to help them meet the expectations themselves in the classroom.

- Establish expectations by asking questions.

Planning and Reflecting

What are your behavioral and social expectations for students? How should they treat one another? How should they treat you and your colleagues? How do you expect students to behave?

_____

_____

_____

What are your academic expectations for students? What should students learn? How should students learn?

_____

_____

_____

How will you model expectations for students?

_____

_____

_____

What will you do for students who struggle to meet expectations? How will you adjust?

_____

_____

_____

_____

Add Your Own SECRET SAUCE Ingredients

Try to boil down your expectations for students into three broad rules—and keep it simple!

1. _____

_____

_____

2. _____

_____

_____

3. _____

_____

_____

A Recipe for Success

Establishing Routines and Procedures

For many teachers, developing high expectations simply begins with establishing familiar routines and procedures.

When my fifth-grade teaching career came to an end, I spent time as a basic skills teacher, supporting students in both in-class and pull-out settings. At the beginning of the year, my role was to assist several fourth-grade students who were struggling with math. The plan was for me to come into the classroom and work with two small groups every day during their forty-minute station time—one group for the first twenty minutes and then the second group for the remaining twenty minutes.

As a classroom teacher, I had never implemented stations particularly well, probably because I was a little impatient, so I watched with interest as my colleague rolled out stations to the students. We spent the first four weeks in September going through the routines. We introduced very little content or instruction during the first two weeks; the students mostly moved to and from the stations around the room and we would model scenarios.

What do you do if you don't have a sharpened pencil?

Where can you find extra paper in the classroom?

What do you do if both you and a classmate arrive at a computer at the same time to use it?

During the next two weeks, some new content was introduced, but we still focused on all the important routines and classroom procedures.

We had originally planned for four weeks of this pattern, and I felt this was plenty. The students had done the rotations over and over again, although there were a few hiccups. When the bell dinged, indicating it was time to move to a new station, most of the students stopped. *Most* of them. The kids were tired of the repetition. I was tired of it. Even my colleague was tired of it; however, she felt one more week would solidify the routines. It was her classroom, so I deferred to her, despite not understanding why we needed to work on the routines for a fifth straight week.

When I asked her, she explained that she had noticed the students were not immediately cleaning up materials at the one-minute warning prior to moving from one station to the next. She had always set up her station rotations this way, and she noticed the slightest hesitation in the way they were cleaning up. Even after four weeks of practicing the routines, the students needed a little more modeling. This part of the routine was key if we were going to transition in a timely manner. So we spent our fifth week in a row working on the routines—and it paid off.

We spent the year doing stations—rotating new content in and having students practice previously learned skills—and I have never seen a classroom run more smoothly! The experience of building routines in this classroom helped me recognize the importance of holding students to high expectations and spending as much time as necessary to build those routines and procedures at the beginning of the year.

It is absolutely *imperative* to make sure students understand the routines inside and out. They must internalize them so their learning process can run on autopilot. Although it can feel like a waste of precious time, the work and time spent at the start of a year or semester is worth it when February or March come around and students know exactly how to do something and have no questions during stations or a collaborative activity.

Try these strategies to ensure routines and procedures are built properly within your classroom:

Practice, practice, and practice again. When routines have been drilled into students, the classroom runs like a fine-tuned machine. Students solve their own problems. They move quickly and efficiently through tasks and rarely need to ask the teacher for help with a logistical issue. This happens through repeated modeling and practice. Students need to follow classroom procedures over and over to ensure they are ingrained in the students' minds. It creates efficiency and establishes purpose. Even after you feel students have the routines down, continue to practice them throughout the year.

Don't assume students know how to do something. Some students may not know what your directions mean. When you tell students to "talk quietly," you may expect them to be at a three out of ten, while the students' understanding of a "quiet voice" can be around an eight out of ten. Expectations at school may be different from expectations at home, or students may not even be expected to talk quietly at home. In these cases, modeling is helpful so all students know what is expected.

Plan for even the smallest details. Don't leave anything to chance. Students want and expect routines and procedures. Knowing exactly how to do things every day gives students a sense of normalcy. Include even the smallest details, such as the examples that follow, in the routines and procedures you build into your class:

- How will students let you know they need to go to the bathroom?
- Where are extra supplies located within the classroom? How do students access them?
- What happens if a child needs a tissue?

- How should a student dispose of garbage or get a drink of water?

So many of these things happen on a regular basis in every classroom. Make sure you have an established plan of action to address these needs so students don't need to waste instructional time thinking about basics.

Place the onus of responsibility on students. You may be lucky and only have a small class of five students, or maybe you work with a group of twenty-five or thirty-six students. No matter how many students you work with, you are still only one person. If you make yourself responsible for every routine and procedure, you simply won't be able to get everything done. It will be nearly impossible to manage every single detail; you will need help. This is where your students come in. Place much of the responsibility on students. Make them accountable for managing basic routines. Teach them to help themselves. Show them the way, then *get out* of their way. Spend your time supporting individual students instead.

Chapter 3

CULTURE

*Students don't care how much
you know until they know
how much you care.*

—JOHN MAXWELL

What You Need to Know: Establishing a positive culture in
your classroom should be a top priority. Give yourself plenty
of time, and make sure students understand the culture and
expectations of your class.

Some teachers work really hard at classroom culture. Some do
not. No matter the amount of effort you put into it, though,
your classroom *will* develop a culture. It might be a positive one
where students feel cared for and supported and where they are
willing to help, share, and collaborate with their peers. Or the
culture could be toxic, sucking the life out of everyone in the
classroom—students *and* teacher. You will struggle to teach, and
your students will struggle to learn. Kids will hate being in your
class, and you will question your ability every day.

Not a Mental Checklist

This is exactly how my first year of teaching began. I was woefully underprepared, though I thought I knew what I was doing. I had a mental checklist, and shortly after being hired, I began to check off items in my head.

I went to the local teacher supply store and bought a number of motivational posters to decorate my classroom.

Check.

I can't tell you today what those posters said, but a colleague had told me to take a picture of the room when I was done so I would know how to set it up the next year—as if my classroom would remain static year after year.

Next, I focused on my lesson plans.

Check.

I poured myself into the content. I spent hours and hours planning and refining my lessons. If I knew one thing, it was this: in order to be successful, I needed a great anticipatory set—or a bell ringer, depending on where you went to school—and some anchor activities. If I could get the students interested in the lesson during the first five minutes, then of course they would remain with me for the duration of the fifty-minute lesson, no questions asked. (How naive I was!)

I developed a foolproof classroom-management "system."

Check.

Actually, I simply decided I needed to dangle some carrots to make kids compliant. I dropped some major coin on my "system" with the bright idea for students to earn daily raffle tickets for their behavior. I would hold a monthly raffle and spend more than $200 on gift cards over the course of the year. Don't ask how many raffle tickets ended up on the floor—or went missing—how much time this took me and the students, or how long students were motivated by the monthly raffles. In case you were wondering, however, one group of students had completely lost interest in the monthly raffle in only one month.

I sent a letter to students and parents to introduce myself. *Check.*

The students and parents knew everything they needed to know about me: where I was from and where I went to school. Done and done. I'm sure the short letter made parents extremely confident and excited about sending their children to learn with me on a daily basis.

I had completed my mental checklist; in my mind, I was ready to be the *awesome* teacher I expected to be. There was just one problem: I didn't really know what I was doing.

Twenty-seven students walked into my classroom on the first day and sized me up. They easily saw through the facade of my nicely decorated classroom. While I did my absolute best for them during those first few months, as I look back, I realize it wasn't good enough. As I said, most of my time was dedicated to lesson planning, learning content, and classroom management. All of the time spent on prep, however, didn't help me manage the classroom. Instead, I was focused on classroom *survival.* I barely made it through each day. Although I would come to rely on a team in later years, I initially believed I had to do it on my own. So I tried to figure it out solo—and failed miserably. Occasionally, I look at parent notes I saved from my first year of teaching. Some addressed the many concerns parents had for their students; some were positive notes, sharing a word of thanks or encouragement. In hindsight, I'm sure the notes of encouragement were written in pity, as parents saw I was in survival mode.

Despite my initial failings as a teacher, I did experience a few bright spots. I worked with one student after school to make sure she got the help necessary for her to improve in math. She had been a struggling fourth-grade student, and her mom knew she needed help right away to break the habit before fifth grade. I agreed and guided her daughter every step of the way. A few students succeeded at learning despite my failed efforts at teaching— mainly because they were compliant, well-behaved students and self-motivated to learn. I'm not sure how much I challenged them to go beyond their limits as a learner. Most of the learning they did was due to their own desire and diligence to learn. They would have been successful with any teacher, but they would have thrived with any *other* teacher (not named Rich)!

What Conversations Are Taking Place in the Faculty Room?

by Trevor Bryan

If you recorded every conversation in the faculty room, what would you hear? Would you hear small talk? Complaining about students? About the curriculum? About professional development? About a new initiative?

Are the conversations mostly positive? Are the conversations mostly negative?

What are colleagues talking about? How are they talking about it? Why are they talking about it?

What are *you* talking about? Are you helping to make things better, or are you fighting for the status quo?

What's your conversation culture? It matters. Probably more than you think it does.

One event during that first year made me realize just how important culture was in my classroom. I never saw it coming, and to this day, it gnaws at me.

The kids *seemed* happy enough. Many lessons didn't go as planned, and I often had to make adjustments for the pace of learning, but the students seemed like they were doing okay. Student behaviors were my biggest concern. I was working with twenty-seven nine- and ten-year-olds. While they had their ups and downs, I was struggling with a particular group of girls. I learned during this first year about the nature of some fifth-grade girls: they use a lot of eye rolls, whisper mean comments under their breath, and fold their arms. On several occasions, I was subjected to the ultimate sign of disrespect from a ten-year-old girl: the dreaded combination of folded arms, mean whispered comments, side-eye, and refusal.

By December, I felt I was doing my best to handle the situation with the girls. I had addressed problems with a group of girls and tried to separate them when there was "mean girl" drama within my classroom. I would keep certain girls separated during class and lunch, but I couldn't help who the girls associated with during recess or on the bus. In my mind, I had done everything I could to minimize the problems.

Then it happened, the situation I never saw coming. In the middle of a random lesson, a little girl burst into tears—uncontrollable sobs. I was helpless. I had no idea how to comfort her. I asked her what was wrong, but she couldn't answer me. I wished she would stop, but she couldn't. Thankfully, I was at least smart enough to walk her into the hallway and ask a passerby to find our guidance counselor to come talk to her. After some investigating from the counselor, I learned the group of mean girls had been bullying her by exclusion. They had left her out of recess games, gotten other girls to exclude her, and completely ignored her on several occasions. Three and a half months into the year, I had no idea any of this was happening. I had no idea how to erase the pain. So much for my happy bunch of students. I had allowed the culture of my classroom to become one in which a girl was crying herself to sleep each night and scared to come to school for fear of what other students in *my* class were going to do to her.

I was devastated. I didn't know how to fix it, but I knew I needed to do something. A few of my colleagues told me it wasn't my fault. I knew they were trying to make me feel better, but ultimately, I knew my complete lack of focus on any type of *culture* had resulted in exactly what I did not want: a toxic, inadequate environment where kids did not feel safe.

Fortunately, the story had a happy ending. I did what I could during the remainder of the school year to improve the classroom culture. It wasn't a quick or easy fix, but by the end of the year, I was able to begin to heal some of the wounds opened during the first months of school. In my second year of teaching, I began incorporating several techniques to allow me to focus on culture from day one. As I progressed through my career, I learned to build a strong, positive culture in the classroom. I worked at it, helped students work at it, and it made all the difference.

Strategies to Address Culture

Whether you are a first-year teacher or starting your twenty-fifth year of teaching, take time *this year* to improve your classroom culture. It can make all the difference for you, as well as your students. Try these strategies for addressing culture:

Simplify the rules in your classroom. Many classrooms contain a list of rules to guide daily interactions. Sometimes students and teachers are beholden to these rules, limiting much-needed flexibility and sometimes not meeting the needs of individual students. There is no list capable of addressing every situation possibly arising in the classroom, so think simple. Find guidelines to work for you and give students a supportive structure they can reference every day. I used the phrase "Be nice. Work hard. Think big," to guide students in my fifth-grade classroom. Specific actions related to these words were modeled for students and referenced when they stepped out of line. Rather than have a hard set of rules and consequences, these broad guiding principles provided flexibility to meet the needs of all students.

Reconsider motivational techniques for students. Many teachers utilize reward systems using points, sticker charts, marbles, clip charts, and other forms of motivational carrots being dangled in front of students. These systems may work for certain students but don't work for every student. (Don't get me started on the public shaming aspect of some of these systems!) When I was in the classroom, I tried a number of these reward systems but had to switch often during the year, especially when students lost interest. I hadn't considered the systems might not work for certain students. We have learned enough about motivation now to know students who are intrinsically motivated are much more likely to succeed in school. Motivate students by engaging them in content and projects they are passionate about. Include student *choice* and *voice* to ensure students are taking ownership for their own learning.

Give everyone what they need. This requires focusing on *equity*, not equality. Whenever one of my own children raises concerns over inequitable treatment, I reply with this simple statement: "There is a big difference in life between what you *want* and what you *need*." Often, children need different things. Some students might need homework in order to practice necessary skills, while other students can skip the homework without suffering academically. Some students might perform better when given an oral assessment versus a written assessment. Still others may be able to demonstrate their learning by completing a performance-based assessment. Some students may require more verbal warnings, while others will only respond to positive reaffirmations. Explain to your students on the first day of school that they will be given what they need but not always equally.

Celebrate everything! Finding ways to celebrate with students builds a positive culture. Some celebrations you can incorporate into your classroom are obvious, such as welcoming students with fanfare on the first day. Give thanks and give back to others during Thanksgiving, or encourage them to create their own Macy's balloons and parade around the building. Welcome students back to school in January with a New Year's bash, complete with air horns, noisemakers, and party hats. More importantly, find opportunities for smaller celebrations. Did a younger student lose her first tooth? Time for some pomp and circumstance! Did a student pass his driver's test? Big opportunity for celebrating! Host a ritual ceremony each time a student completes a rite of passage, or create your own reasons to celebrate. International Talk Like a Pirate Day? Absolutely. Eye patches and *arrgghhhhs*! Roll out the red carpet—literally!—when welcoming a new student or staff member, or when saying goodbye. Red butcher paper works great during a Clap-In (welcome) or Clap-Out (goodbye). No matter what the occasion, find a way to bring positivity and fun to what you do each day!

Recognize the power of the class meeting. Take a few minutes each morning, or sit down as a group once a week for twenty minutes, to meet, discuss, and share. Meeting time can be used to model expectations for interacting with one another, to help solve problems or address conflicts within the classroom, and ultimately, to celebrate one another's successes. The class meeting provides an opportunity to build culture through community. It will help you and your students grow closer, share in joy, and sympathize or commiserate when necessary. Taking just a few minutes away from instruction each week can pay dividends in the long run and eliminate the potential for problems to grow if not addressed. While it might seem counterintuitive, the time spent will be well worth it if it leads to a stronger learning community and culture within your classroom.

A Five-Day Plan to Build or Improve Classroom Culture

Day 1: Hold a class meeting. Announce the importance of collaboration and problem-solving. Model some student-interaction strategies reinforcing this notion. Teach students how to use Rock-Paper-Scissors as the ultimate tool to settle differences. Two students arguing over a seat? Rock-Paper-Scissors. Two students in a disagreement over group work? Rock-Paper-Scissors.

Day 2: Hold a discussion about expectations. Let students know your expectations and ask them what theirs are. Talk about how you can meet their expectations and what they can do to help one another satisfy classroom expectations. Allow them to have a voice in the discussion. Explain the supports you will put in place to help students succeed in meeting expectations.

Day 3: Model ownership practices. Explain to students that the classroom is as much theirs as it is yours. Model more strategies and routines to help students gain independence. You could build routines for students to answer basic questions for one another if you are not available to meet with them, for example. "Ask Three, Then Me" is a great strategy to accomplish this. Students who don't know how to do something, need help, or have a basic question need to ask three other students before they interrupt the teacher. Show them simple routines for accomplishing basic tasks in the classroom, such as requesting bathroom breaks, finding a new pencil or other supplies, and moving to another activity when they finish an assignment.

Day 4: Hold a class meeting and fix a problem. Start the meeting by saying, "I notice we are struggling with _____. How can we fix this?" List all student responses and talk through the positives and negatives. Make a decision everyone in the classroom can and will live by.

Day 5: Celebrate early successes. Don't place the emphasis on points, rewards, or clip charts. Rather, celebrate and highlight when students are collaborating or helping one another. Explain how student interactions can improve the classroom environment. Give students the chance to celebrate one another. Remember to include anyone who participates in your learning space, like another teacher or an instructional aide. They should also be recognized and given the chance to share during your class meeting.

After those first five days, continue to use mini-lessons and the class meeting to model, problem-solve, and celebrate. Culture within a classroom is constantly growing, so make it a focus as you move forward! Take every opportunity to focus on culture. Students not being nice to one another? Stop immediately and address the situation. Bring it up again during your weekly or daily meeting, and model expectations for students. Don't assume culture can be built in two weeks and magically maintained

> throughout the year. Culture is built continually and improved upon each day; however, while culture can't be built in a day, it *can* be destroyed in a day. Don't ever forget that, and continue to work at it each day!

Never forget culture will develop in your classroom whether you focus on it or completely ignore it. Both new *and* experienced teachers make the mistake of focusing a great deal of time and energy on lesson plans, classroom management, and other everyday minutiae. I see clip charts, points systems, and other management strategies used to keep students compliant, obedient, and on task; I even used some of these systems in my own classroom. I quickly realized, though, that even the best laid plans will be derailed promptly if the culture of the classroom is not positive. Don't make this mistake. Focus every day on culture!

SECRET SAUCE SUMMARY

- Focusing on culture in your classroom can help you develop a positive culture. Ignoring it can lead to a negative or toxic culture.

- Simplify your rules in the classroom. Use broad, guiding principles rather than a limiting set of rules.

- Reconsider motivational techniques for students. Reward systems can work in certain situations and for certain students, but the results can be short-lived. Avoid extrinsic rewards and prizes; shoot for intrinsic motivators to get students to care.

- Find opportunities to celebrate in your classroom. Celebrate individual students, holidays, rites of passage, and made-up holidays. Any reason to honor and praise should be recognized.
- Use class meetings to discuss, share, celebrate, and problem-solve with students.

Planning and Reflecting

How do you actively support the culture in your classroom? What are the guiding principles you want your classroom culture to be built upon?

_____

_____

_____

What type of behavior management system do you use—or intend to use—in your classroom? Is it based on intrinsic or extrinsic motivators? If extrinsic, how can you modify it?

_____

_____

_____

How can you gather student feedback on a regular basis to improve your classroom culture?

_____

_____

_____

In what classroom or school have you seen an extremely positive culture? What did the educators and students do to create and maintain such a positive culture?

_____

_____

_____

Add Your Own SECRET SAUCE Ingredients

List three actions you will take to improve the culture in your classroom or school.

1. _____

_____

_____

2. _____

_____

_____

3. _____

_____

_____

A Recipe for Success

#GoodNewsPhoneCall

While I've heard this advice for years, I've found very few teachers who participate in positive phone calls to their students' homes. Calling home for a good reason early on helps establish a positive relationship between teacher and parent. If you then have to make a call home for a behavioral or academic concern, having already established a positive relationship will make the phone call easier.

As a building principal, I have started making a #GoodNewsPhoneCall home when students do something note-worthy—perhaps an academic achievement or an act of kindness. Regardless of the reason, the parents' surprise always comes across the phone line. The conversations usually sound like this:

> *Good afternoon! This is Mr. Czyz calling, and I have Dante in my office.*
>
> *Is everything okay? What's wrong? Is Dante in some sort of trouble?*
>
> *Actually, we are calling with a "good news phone call." Dante was a great friend today during lunch when he helped a classmate clean up his spilled lunch. Dante even offered to share his own lunch with his friend. We are very proud of Dante, as I'm sure you are, too.*
>
> *[Silence]*

Eventually the parents respond, usually overwhelmed with joy and pride, and sometimes with tears. At this point, I usually give the receiver to the student so they can talk to their mom or dad or other special adult. As excited as I am to tell the parents what the students did, my favorite part is watching the students talk to their parents. They are beaming with pride!

After we finish these phone calls, the student and I take a picture together. I share it on our school's social media accounts so everyone can hear the good news, and then I add the student's name to our #GoodNewsPhoneCall Wall of Fame located in our main office. This is probably one of the most rewarding parts of my job. It doesn't matter if the student is in kindergarten or fifth grade. Every one of them walks around with the biggest smile for the rest of the day! I've even talked to teachers and administrators at the middle and high schools who receive the same reactions from older students when they call home for positive reasons.

Chapter 4

RELATIONSHIPS

My students don't need me to learn.
They need me to care.

—LIZ GALARZA, MIDDLE SCHOOL
TEACHER IN NEW YORK

What You Need to Know: Building relationships is the single most important action you will take as an educator. Forming positive relationships with all stakeholders will allow you to get to know who you are working with and what drives them.

I'm going to let you in on a little secret: this is the most important chapter in the book. It is the most vital ingredient to the SECRET SAUCE. It's going to make all the difference.

What I'm about to tell you is actually all you truly need to be successful in your career. In fact, I probably could have written a picture book with just these simple pieces of advice.

If you want to be a successful educator, all you need to know is just a few words away. I wanted to be careful about putting this too early in the book because I didn't want you to put the book down once you learned it!

This is exactly what held me up while writing this book. If I'm going to give away the magic formula to teaching, I need to make sure you are on the edge of your seat, on the verge of standing up at any moment and shouting:

> *What is it, Rich? What is going to make me the best teacher I can be? What is the vital SECRET SAUCE ingredient to make me a successful educator? How can I become the best I can be?*

I assure you—it really is very simple. Are you ready?

Okay. Here we go. These are three *most* important things you need to do as an educator:

Build relationships.

Build relationships.

And, wait for it…

BUILD RELATIONSHIPS.

In case you are not quite following yet, the most important thing you can do as an educator is to *build relationships*—relationships with *students*, relationships with *colleagues*, relationships with *parents*.

Start with Students

Build relationships with everyone you come in contact with each day, but start with students.

As a teacher, the best part of my day was connecting with students. It didn't matter how we connected; just sharing a connection was important. I usually learned something the student was really interested in and shared my personal interest in the same thing. I connected with many students through a shared love of sports. One year I had a student who was a hockey player and a huge fan of the New Jersey Devils. When he first walked into my classroom and saw the Devils Stanley Cup banner hanging on the wall, I was instantly likable to him, and he was able to trust me. My co-teacher was also a hockey fan but rooted for the New York Rangers. The friendly rivalry we had during the year helped me and my colleague build a strong relationship with the student. Our almost daily discussions about hockey helped my co-teacher engage our student in learning, as well. At the end of the year, the student even asked his mom to purchase personalized hockey jerseys for us. I still have my "Czyz #1" Devils jersey, and it reminds me of the power of building strong relationships with students.

I also enjoyed connecting with students over our love of books. When several of my students were reading *Holes* by Louis Sachar, I read it over our winter break so I could share in their daily conversations. I finished the book while sitting on a comfy chair at a relative's house on Christmas Eve and didn't move for three hours. I'm not sure my family was entirely happy about the fact that I didn't speak to anyone during the day, but I just couldn't put the book down! It remains one of my favorite books, and I can still remember the conversations I shared with students when we returned in the new year.

Building relationships is about getting to know your students. You need to show them you care about them, first and foremost, as a person. You need to learn as much about them as possible. Just be careful when listening to colleagues share their opinions of students. In my first role as a teacher, each team of grade-level teachers worked with the building administration to place students in new classes for the following year. We noted students' strengths, as well as their specific needs. Administrators then worked with our guidance counselor to create tentative class lists for the following school year. The final step of this process was a shared grade-level meeting where the fourth- and fifth-grade teachers met to review the lists. The fourth-grade teachers checked the lists to see if they had any concerns and were also able to provide insight to each fifth-grade teacher about their classes. I dreaded the meeting; it was one of the worst grade-level meetings I had to participate in each year.

While I understood the thinking behind it, in practice, the meeting usually devolved into a list of complaints and negative comments about some of the students. The negativity was usually couched as some sort of positive advice about the student: "Be sure not to sit him anywhere near your desk. He can be really annoying," or "She's a great student, but she often refuses to do her work and can be really difficult to work with." This always bothered me for a number of reasons, primarily because a teacher should never openly complain about a student to another teacher, especially one who has yet to meet the student. It's for this same reason the faculty room can have such negative energy. As a teacher, I always wanted to meet students and learn about them myself without anyone else's bias informing my judgment. Students deserve a fresh start every day. Some students described to me as "annoying" or "difficult to work with" actually ended up being some of my favorite students, simply because I took the time to get to know them, to build relationships with them, to understand where they were coming from, and to provide scaffolds to support them.

#DitchTheClips
by Elizabeth Merce, @EMercedLearning

One of the biggest tips new teachers get from veteran teachers is that classroom management is the most important thing you need to master. Unfortunately, even the best teacher-prep programs are focused more on content delivery and supports, including external reinforcements for behavioral modification, such as those awful clip chart systems—or even worse, reinforcement through candy and food. Still more concerning is how these clip charts are often used to publicly shame our most fragile learners. Many educators have realized external rewards and public call-outs are not the solution for management issues.

When you take the step to Ditch the Clips, you need to commit to knowing what developmental stages your students are in and how this impacts their learning. It means knowing how to teach peripheral skills, such as those related to self-help, or social, emotional, and meta-cognitive skills. Teaching the whole child means knowing where children are in the development of those skills and scaffolding their growth in those areas with as much intention as you would an academic skill.

How do you know each child's skill level? Through relationships. When you build relationships with your students, you begin to see everything differently. You begin to see them as individuals, not as members of your "class." Master teachers weave this relationship and skill-building into content instruction so seamlessly they often forget they are doing it. Novice teachers feel disadvantaged,

> believing there is a magic formula when, in reality, the formula is simply getting to know students as people and building these soft skills along with academic skills. Let's #DitchTheClips and build relationships and skills instead. I promise you won't be disappointed.

Building Relationships with Students

So how do you get to know your students and start to build powerful relationships? Start with these time-tested methods:

Greet every student every day. Start each day at your classroom door, greeting students by name as they enter the room. You won't be able to get to know your students until you can call them by name. Regardless of how many students you work with each day—ten, twenty-five, or 125—it's imperative to call each one by name. Names are so important. Make sure you are pronouncing names correctly, too. Getting to know students starts with calling them by the right names—and doing so daily. Some teachers develop a personal handshake with each student they teach; some come up with nicknames for students. One year, I had two girls in my class named Courtney. One of the girls suggested I call her "Court" for short. It stuck, but not in the way she intended. For the rest of the year, she was "Court for Short," and she loved it! No matter how you do it, make sure you connect with each student every day. It helps them know they are cared for.

Use interest surveys. At the beginning of the year, start learning everything you can about your students: their likes, dislikes, interests, passions, allergies, biggest influences, etcetera. Find out their favorite—or least favorite—foods, books, movies, video games, or YouTube channels. Anything you learn about a student is invaluable and will help you make a stronger connection.

Interest surveys are an easy way to do this. If you work with young students, send home a paper copy of an interest survey so parents can provide information about their children. If you work with older students, use a simple paper copy students can fill out during the first week of class or use a Google form to keep the information in one place.

Let students in. As important as it is for you to learn about students, it is equally important for students to learn about *you*. Don't be afraid to share your passions, your strengths and areas for improvement, your likes and dislikes, etcetera. When I first started teaching, my mentor told me I needed to "add my personality" to my interactions each day to become a better teacher. I wasn't sure what she meant until I realized the powerful connections I started to make with students once I shared things with them—pictures, details about my family, and my interests outside of school. One of the most powerful connections I made with students grew by sharing music throughout our day. They were always interested to hear what new music I might be listening to or hear me play in the classroom music they were familiar with. "Oh, my parents listen to this" was always a common refrain, though I'm not sure it was meant as a compliment! Students appreciated that I, too, was a real person, someone who went to the grocery store, someone who listened to some of the same music and read some of the same books.

Engage in a meaningful conversation (or two, or five, or ten) every day. As you've just learned, connecting with every student every day is important. Engaging in meaningful discussions with students every day is also important. While you won't be able to talk to everyone in this manner each day, make sure you check in with all your students over the span of a week or a few weeks. Meaningful conversations might include why a student is struggling in another class or might be about a student's upcoming dance recital or art show. Again, it doesn't matter what you are talking about as long as it's an authentic interaction showing you care about the student. If you are able to have one of these conversations each day, great! If you are able to have two, even better! Five to ten? *Perfect!* The key is to have as many important and worthwhile conversations as possible, with as many students as possible, each day. No conversations or interactions are wasted because they allow you to constantly work on building better relationships.

Establish trust (and try never to break that trust!). It is very difficult to establish trust with every student. It takes a *lot* of work. Based on their previous school experiences, some students will automatically trust you while others will automatically distrust you. You will have to work at building a relationship based on trust with both groups of students. This can be incredibly difficult, and unfortunately, once you have put in the time and effort to establish that trust, it is extremely easy to break it. Once a student loses trust, regaining it is even harder. Be open and honest with students. Explain your *why*. Give them every reason to trust you, and *always* follow through on your word, even when it is difficult.

Relationships with Colleagues

Much of what you just read about building successful relationships with students also applies to your relationships with the other adults at your school or in your district. Engaging in meaningful conversations, building (and never losing) trust, and sharing your story can help establish solid relationships. Additional steps can strengthen bonds as well, and limit the negativity potentially creeping into your working relationships.

Be open, honest, and transparent—always. Just as you expect your students to do, keep the truth at the forefront of everything you do. Be open and honest in your interactions with others, and be transparent about the motivations behind the decisions you make. If you make a mistake, fess up and move forward. Lying, stretching the truth, or intentionally leaving out key details will only strain your relationships. The truth, however, will set you free!

Avoid the rumor mill. Want to avoid some negativity? Along with always telling the truth, one of the most important acts you can take is to stay away *completely* from the rumor mill. Some of your colleagues might love to spread and revel in gossip: "Did you hear what happened to [insert name here]? I heard he or she had to speak with a supervisor because an angry parent called the superintendent!" Unfortunately, these types of conversations can lead to hurt feelings and uneasy interactions, and they often make it awkward for others trying to mind their own business. Avoid getting involved.

Show appreciation. Sometimes working in education can be a lonely experience. Many great things educators do are often overlooked and unsung. Be sure you show appreciation for those around you. You might make the simple gesture of buying a cup of coffee for your building secretary when you pick up your own morning java, or simply take a moment to recognize another's act of kindness. In my school, we honor students each month for their growth in social-emotional learning. At the same time, we take care to recognize one another with a few kind words and a certificate granting a simple reward like a free dress-down day, a GOOSE Pass (**G**et **O**ut **o**f **S**chool Thirty Minutes Early), or a free coverage period. A simple act like this goes a long way to show your colleagues they are appreciated for what they do.

Be observant and attentive. Take notice of those around you. Did the teacher in the classroom across the hall, who normally shows up an hour early each morning, suddenly arrive late each day for the past week? Stop by and ask if everything is okay. Do you notice a colleague struggling with a particular student frequently? Offer allowing the student to visit your classroom for a much-needed break. Watch to see when a colleague might be out of sorts, and do your best to encourage him or her regardless of the issue. Showing you notice and, more importantly, that you *care*, can strengthen your relationships with the other adults around you.

Collaborate and share. Some teachers want to close their doors and do everything on their own. They are unwilling to share or collaborate, and they especially don't want you to "steal" their lessons or project ideas. The most effective teachers, however, share with and borrow from one another. They realize the power in collaborating. Planning with someone else can ease the burden of doing it alone and can invigorate your lessons. *Exceptional* teachers solicit feedback from colleagues and use the constructive criticism to improve their instruction. They seek constant improvement, and one of the best ways to do this is to learn and grow together.

Be positive–always. The world offers plenty to complain about, so being negative is extremely easy. The only problem is, no one really wants to listen. Some may tolerate doing so, but they are secretly lamenting how the speaker is *way too negative*. More importantly, you need to model positivity for your students. Be the positive one. Share and spread positivity. When something goes wrong, find the silver lining. Talk about the great things students are doing instead of the not-so-great things. Share the stories about the parents who are making a positive impact on their children. Positivity begets positivity. When enough adults promote a positive culture in your school, it will also spread to students and drown out the negativity.

Each time you have a positive interaction with someone, you are building positive relationships. Whether with a student, colleague, or parent (more on this soon!), the time you spend cultivating and strengthening relationships will only help you as an educator—and more importantly, as a human being. Relationships are the cornerstone of your success as a teacher. Everything positive you experience as a teacher will be built upon your ability to foster relationships. Create those relationships. Connect and share. Nurture your relationships, and let people know you care. It will carry you a long way in your educational career.

SECRET SAUCE SUMMARY

- Building relationships is one of the most important steps you can take to help your students learn.

- Start by greeting students each day and recognize the importance of names. Greet students by their names and show them you care.

- Survey students—and possibly parents—to find out likes, dislikes, hobbies, interests, passions, strengths, areas for growth, and anything else that would help you establish a better relationship with students.

- Share yourself with your students. Let them know your likes, dislikes, and passions. Show them you are a real person, too, and worthy of building a relationship with.

- Engage in meaningful conversations with students every day to build and strengthen your relationships.

- Build—and never break—trust with students. If you do break it, own it and work to rebuild it.

- Be honest and transparent with colleagues. Avoid getting involved with rumors, gossip, and hearsay.

- Show appreciation for your colleagues.

- Pay attention to your colleagues. Be observant so you can recognize when someone is struggling. In those moments, be supportive.

- Be willing to collaborate and share with colleagues. Everyone can grow together!
- Always stay positive in your conversations and actions.

Planning and Reflecting

What actions do you take to actively build, maintain, and support relationships with those around you?

_____

_____

_____

How can you improve your relationships with students, colleagues, and parents?

_____

_____

_____

Do you engage in positivity or negativity in your daily interactions? If some, or even most, of your interactions are negative, how can you flip them to be more positive?

_____

_____

_____

How do you share yourself with your students? What do your students know about you? What else can you share so they know you better?

_____

_____

_____

Count the number of meaningful conversations you have with students each day. Where can you find time to engage in more conversations with students?

_____

_____

_____

Add Your Own SECRET SAUCE Ingredients

List three actions you will take to build and improve relationships.

1. _____

_____

_____

2. _____

_____

_____

3. _____

_____

_____

A Recipe for Success

Building Positive Relationships with Parents, Guardians, and Families

Parents are an educator's greatest ally, and yet educators often dismiss parents' actions or deflect their interest and support. It is incumbent upon every single educator to build strong, positive relationships with families—starting with their first interaction. Whether you are meeting a parent face-to-face for the first time or sending a letter to each family before the school year begins, setting the right tone is important. Parents or guardians usually have a short list of expectations: they want to know you care for their child, will keep their child safe in your classroom, and will do your best to help their child learn. How you interact with parents from the beginning can help establish a beautiful working relationship where everyone is engaged to ensure the students get exactly what they need.

I recently met a teacher who had taught multiple siblings— seven over approximately twenty years. The parents of these children always advocated to ensure their children were placed in this teacher's classroom. They trusted the teacher because of the relationship she had built with them over the years. Every parent or guardian deserves this, and it begins with *your* communication.

Start with a handwritten letter or note. A family who receives a personalized note shortly before school begins already knows you care. They know you are making the extra effort to reach out, and it's a powerful message even before day one! Writing notes to all your students' families may seem difficult or incredibly time-consuming, but the energy and time you expend will be well worth it. If you have your class roster(s) during the summer, write several notes a week. If you try to write them all at once, it will be overwhelming and unmanageable.

Take advantage of every opportunity. You may work in a school where you have frequent opportunities for parent engagement, or you may be in a setting where you don't often have the chance for face-to-face interaction with parents. Regardless of your situation, take advantage of every opportunity to connect with parents. When I first started teaching, I worked in an elementary building where thirty buses rolled in every morning and afternoon. There were no sidewalks near the building, so most students were dropped off and picked up by bus. We didn't have many opportunities to see parents. A few years later, while working at another school in the district, I had the firsthand opportunity to see parent interaction at its best. Most parents (or other family members) walked their children to and from the school. Everyone converged on the blacktop in the morning, and teachers had daily interactions with parents. If there was a concern during the day, staff knew they could talk to a parent at the end of the day during pick-up time. Your setting may not include opportunities like this, but find those moments where you can connect with parents. It could be at an after-school sporting event or when a parent comes to pick up their child early. Use old-fashioned forms of communication, too, like phone calls home (positive ones too!), weekly newsletters (hard copy or digital), and handwritten notes.

Help parents ask the right questions. As a parent, I've experienced asking the wrong questions to my kids about school, such as "How was school?" followed by a curt "Fine." Or "What did you do at school today?" followed by the universal student response, "Nothing." Help families avoid these situations by providing a list of question prompts or topics they can talk about with their students. Share a daily photo from your classroom, encouraging parents to ask a specific question, like *Ask students to describe our science experiment today* or *Have students explain the impact of the civil rights movement on later generations.* Any guidance you provide can help parents and caregivers connect with what is happening in their students' daily lives.

Reach parents where they are. The explosion of technology tools and social media has made communicating with families incredibly easy. You can now instant message parents and receive a message back within minutes, all while you are in class with their children. You can connect with parents on any number of social media platforms or technology tools, but the key is determining their preferences and what forms of communication they are most comfortable with. Start the school year with a simple questionnaire, asking them for their preferred mode of communication. Some parents may prefer phone calls; some may be easier to reach via e-mail. Some may prefer a text message or direct message via an app. Ask them. Find out what is easiest for them and then use their preferred method to ensure you reach them on a regular basis.

Engage parents who can't attend events. Some parents want to participate in their child's education but cannot for any number of reasons. They may be working at a time when other parents are able to be involved. They may come from a culture or family in which participation in school events is not the norm. They may not have transportation to get to school. Instead of judging parents for their inability to participate in school-based events like parent-teacher conferences, evening concert performances, or family curriculum nights, find a way to include them. While preparing for our school's winter concert one year, a parent e-mailed to ask if I would be livestreaming the event for parents who could not attend. He would be traveling on business and unable to be present at the performance. Even though I hadn't planned on it, and wasn't quite sure how to do it, I assured him I would livestream portions of the concert. I spent the rest of the afternoon figuring out the logistics and what tool would be best for sharing the performance. The next day, I received an e-mail from the parent expressing his gratitude. In addition, several other parents and extended family members who hadn't been able to attend *were* able to share in the performance by watching the livestream.

Find similar ways to include parents who may have difficulty participating. Share photos or videos of student performances. Record and share informational sessions. Host events at times when most parents can attend and find alternative times for other parents. Offer several sessions sharing the same information. Connect for a parent-teacher conference via phone or video chat. Seek out additional opportunities for families to get involved in their student's education.

Host a Family Camp event. The success of the Edcamp movement has revolutionized professional learning for educators. For those who have not attended an Edcamp, it is a professional learning opportunity for educators that is completely driven by the participants. Teachers choose what sessions they will attend and what topics they will discuss. Use this powerful concept to impact and engage families in the education process. Find an open Saturday and bring parents, students, and teachers together to share and learn. Coordinate activities families can participate in together like STEM challenges, Hack-A-Thons (coding), or community-based problem-solving. Share curriculum information sessions and resources with parents such as "How Am I Supposed to Help My Child with Math Homework?!?!" or "Reading Strategies You Can Use at Home." Let parents share their expertise by leading a session like "Simple Healthy Meal Ideas for Kids" or "Organizing Your Family and Your Life." Include community organizations and take advantage of community partnerships. Ask local law enforcement to share information about internet safety and online citizenship for students. Invite local yoga instructors to lead sessions on mindfulness and breathing exercises. Organize play areas for kids to have fun while parents learn.

Most importantly, make sure you feed everyone involved. Work with local businesses who will donate bagels and coffee in the morning, and pizza or sandwiches in the afternoon. Find a local shop to come prepare fruit smoothies or dessert for your participants. Make the day fun and engaging so everyone involved learns something new and appreciates the importance of being a constant and continuous learner.

Listen to understand, not to respond. Effectively communicating with parents and guardians means you will sometimes need to have difficult conversations with them. It may be in regard to a discipline issue or academic concern you are having. It may be connected to a parent calling you out on a mistake you made. When these crucial, arduous, or fierce conversations with a parent are necessary, make sure you are listening *to understand* and not listening to respond. In many cases, parents just want to know you understand their perspectives. They may simply need to vent or be heard. They may not be looking for a solution; they may only want to share how they or their child feels about something. Try to avoid getting defensive or placing judgment during these conversations. Respect and empathize with the parents. Try to walk in their shoes. Listen to understand. Parents may have different experiences than you do. Try to settle on an agreement beneficial for everyone but, most importantly, one most beneficial for the student involved.

Send parents a weekly newsletter or video message created by students. Parents will tune in if their children are involved. Ask students to share a weekly newsletter or video message about what they have been learning throughout the week. Recently, a colleague of mine gave students the opportunity to create a weekly newsletter through Smore.com. During the initial stages, she simply showed students how to add information to the online newsletter, then let them venture out on their own. When set up as an independent writing center in the classroom, it allows students to document their learning on a daily basis. They record experiences, take pictures, share reflections, and at the end of the week, make final edits before they post a link on the class social media page on Friday afternoon. The newsletter is completely student driven and gives parents an impressive glimpse into the classroom. Another option would be to have students record videos using a device and sharing the recordings with families. Or you could video a reflection from a lesson, a weekly wondering in which students ask questions about topics they may be pondering, or a short presentation of something they just learned. Students love creating videos in this manner, and families love seeing their students as the star of the show in your classroom!

Organize learning lunches with community experts. Many parents and other community members have expertise in a variety of areas. Take advantage of this! You may have parents who are published authors or book editors. Some may be authorities with local volunteer organizations who may be able to help with service learning. Perhaps others are artists or singers who can share their experiences with students. Seek out those with talents and specialized skills to help students learn. We recently invited a parent to school who is part of a specialized K-9 unit with local law enforcement and works every day with a dog trained in search and rescue. Students prepared for the visit by learning about specific dog breeds, as well as canine-employed search-and-rescue techniques. They were able to share what they learned and see it in action during the classroom visits. The K-9 team, comprising a human officer and a canine officer, showed students how the dog searches for missing people and even let several students hide in various spots around the school building as the dog proved his skills in finding them. It was a worthwhile endeavor for everyone involved.

Another great option is to set up a learning lunch in which small groups of students can lunch with a community expert—listening, asking questions, and learning. You could find a local artist who can teach students to draw or a local musician willing to share musical techniques and inspiration.

Chapter 5

ERRORS

*Anyone who has never made a mistake
has never tried anything new.*

—ALBERT EINSTEIN

What You Need to Know: Teachers make mistakes and need
to model making mistakes, as well as reflection, for students.
Encouraging mistakes, failing forward (growth through reflection
and adjustments after failure), and learning from errors
can help students develop persistence and promote deeper
learning and growth from reflection.

Model Mistake-Making

How many mistakes have you made as an educator?

If you are relatively new to teaching, you may have spent some
time in the classroom during a field experience or student teaching
placement. How many mistakes did you make during this time?

Ten? Twenty-five? One hundred? Five hundred? One thousand?

If you are an experienced educator who has spent a few years
in the classroom or has worked with students for many years,

think about the number of mistakes or errors you have made during your career.

One thousand? Ten thousand? One hundred thousand? One million?

It is impossible to remember them all. The minor ones have likely been forgotten over time. Some of the major ones may still sting, but probably led you to some important learning after a great deal of reflection. Even after all of those mistakes, you have survived. You are still an educator—one who has learned from your mistakes and improved because of them.

When I was in the classroom, I was fortunate to teach two groups of fifth-grade students each day. I felt bad for the morning students because they were always in my test classes. I used to refer to the morning sessions as the "mistake" lessons for the day. I taught my first math and science lessons of the day and discovered what worked and didn't work. Of course, the classes were different based on specific student needs, but the "mistake" lessons in the morning gave me a chance to explore how to teach content. I always felt my afternoon lessons went better because I was able to reflect quickly on the morning sessions. As a result, I usually had a pretty good idea what common misconceptions the afternoon students would have. Because of this, I could often frontload those lessons with some things to look out for. The opportunity for a redo each day made me a better teacher because it made me think about exactly what I was doing in my lessons.

Going back to the advice I was given when I first began my career—*effective teachers don't make mistakes*—I can say firsthand this is simply not true. Effective educators *do* make mistakes. So do novice teachers and expert teachers. Everyone makes mistakes. Everyone *should* make mistakes. Without them, we wouldn't grow as educators. The important part of making mistakes is being able to reflect upon them and grow from them, both as a teacher *and* as a learner.

Strategies to Create a Culture of Mistake-Making in the Classroom

- **Teach students about those who have failed**. Show students it is okay to fail. Teach them about all the people who had to fail in order to succeed. Give specific examples students can relate to, like Michael Jordan or Walt Disney, and show them how failure can often lead to success.

- **Model and create a resume of failure**. A professor from Princeton University recently shared a list of his failures, which included *degree programs [he] did not get into*, *academic positions [he] did not get*, and *awards and scholarships [he] did not get*. Create your own resume of failures. Show students how, despite setbacks, they can eventually be successful if they reflect and learn from their mistakes. Model your resume for students and encourage them to list their failures along with their eventual successes.

- **Let students create mistakes**. Multiple-choice questions containing four answers usually include three incorrect choices. In an effort to help students think about mistakes, ask them to create four multiple-choice answers to a question. Students should generate the correct answer and three answers containing some sort of error. To do this, they will need to anticipate the mistakes they could make, and over time, those potential mistakes will become nothing more than a tool to get to the correct answer.

- **Ask open-ended questions without a correct answer**. Many of the questions we used to ask students—and sometimes still do—can now easily be found with a simple Google search. Mistakes and errors will become more acceptable when lessons place less emphasis on students getting the right answer and focus more on learning. Start asking questions that don't have just one correct answer. Find open-ended questions requiring multiple solutions.

- **Create an "epic fail" board**. Put all of your mistakes on display—your students' *and* yours. Have students post their mistakes and how it led them to solving a problem or discovering something new. Place your own epic fails alongside theirs, as well as the epic fails of famous people. Show everyone that you and your students embrace mistakes as part of the process of moving forward.

Try these approaches to ensure the mistakes you make become a part of your growth process as an educator, as well as part of a healthy environment for your students.

Show Students It Is Okay to Make Mistakes

When you make a mistake, own up to it. Point it out to students. Teach them mistakes are part of the process. In a kindergarten class, I once watched as a teacher fumbled through spelling a word aloud to show students how figuring out the letters and sounds is part of the process, and everyone, including the teacher, makes mistakes when they are trying to learn. In this environment, you will never hear students tease one another for making mistakes. It's just part of the learning process. So highlight your mistakes. Make some intentional errors. Model for students how they can learn and grow from their mistakes in any content area.

Model your writing process for students. Show them what it looks like to use a specific word, second-guess the word choice, reread the sentence, and then replace the word with another one. Some students will not write for fear of making a mistake. Demonstrate that writing well does not mean the writer is perfect. Show students the process is fraught with errors; everyone makes mistakes throughout the writing process! Model what it looks like to be a *writer*.

Illustrate inevitable mistakes by trying to work through a science experiment. Model by following a procedure and showing how, even if you follow the procedure step-by-step, the actual results may vary from the theoretical results. Demonstrate how it may take several attempts before you get the outcome you expected.

Lead students through the design process. Teach them about the minimum viable product (MVP) technique, in which product designers will release a product that is not fully developed yet in order to learn from users what improvements are needed. Having students participate in a design loop can show them the power of making mistakes, owning them, and revising because of them.

Reflect upon Your Own Mistakes

Those who do not learn from history are doomed to repeat it. The first step when you make a mistake—or a dozen mistakes—is admitting them. It's usually pretty easy to tell when you make a mistake. You finish your forty-five-minute lesson and immediately face the cold, hard truth: *Well, that did not go well!* The mistakes are usually obvious, or you will be able to tell by student responses, that it didn't go well. Are you staring at a sea of fifteen blank faces at the end of a lesson? If so, chances are you can make improvements the next time you work with this group of students. Think about what worked and didn't work. Think about the *why* behind a mistake. Ask yourself questions: *Why didn't students immediately get it? What could I have done differently? How could I have taken a different approach?* Consider the following suggestions as ways to reflect on your mistakes.

Join in a "reflection walkabout" to start or end your week. James Moffett, a former principal at Derby Hills Elementary School in Kansas, and the Derby Hills staff gathered on Friday afternoons, paired off, and walked around the building, reflecting upon their week. Staff can start with two simple questions:

- What went well?
- What didn't go well?

Start a reflection journal. Write about the lessons or activities that do not work out exactly as planned. Jot down a few notes about what you can change to improve the next time. List ideas about how to change your classroom, instruction, or workflow for the following year. Find a way to document what you learned from the mistakes you make in order to become a better educator.

Reflect with students. Involving students in the reflection process is the most powerful activity tied to learning from mistakes. Share your own reflections with students as they reflect on their learning. At the end of the day, circle up with students and share a mistake you made. Talk about what you learned from it and how you plan to fix it next time. Allow students the opportunity to do the same. By modeling mistakes—and more importantly *growth*—you will give students a powerful opportunity for reflection.

Focus on the Process, Not the End Product

Too often students are asked to focus on the final product. For far too many years, our education system has placed emphasis on proving learning: learn, learn, learn, learn, prove learning. In an elementary setting, this focus might appear in the weekly reading cycle. The basal story is read aloud on Monday, and students read independently on Tuesday, followed by more rereads, several discussions, and a few worksheets later in the week. Friday is always the "prove learning" portion, when students take the comprehension test. Many students, through sheer listening comprehension as they hear the story a few times during the week, can do fairly well on the multiple choice part of the test. Their final score on the test then has nothing to do with their actual reading ability, and in this type of cycle, the student has done no work to move forward as a reader.

At the secondary level, it might be a similar path, in which the focus is on the summative assessment pieces like quiz scores, test scores, chapter averages, etcetera. At the end of the chapter, the teacher deems a student knows 80 percent of the material because he or she did poorly on the first quiz but rebounded on the chapter test. Even though the student mastered most of the skills as part of the content, the focus is not on the learning taking place. Instead, it is on the final score. Each student becomes a number: *you earned an 87.6 in US history.*

Instead of focusing on the "learn, learn, learn, learn, prove learning" model, educators need to focus on the process. Teachers need to give students the chance to try, fail, try again, learn, research, try something else, and then share their learning. I like to think of it as Stumble, Fall, Rise, Repeat.

Focus on open-ended questions. Stop asking questions requiring a singular, correct, or defined answer. Instead ask questions with multiple answers. Better yet, ask questions inspiring *more* questions. Give students the opportunity to get lost in the process of trying to find an answer. Once students find an answer, challenge them to find another answer. A great deal of learning takes place this way. Create opportunities for students to be more involved in the process instead of just finding the "correct" answer.

Concentrate on soft skills. Build a classroom environment that encourages creativity, resilience, empathy, perseverance, divergent thinking, etcetera. Allowing students to toil in the learning process requires you to emphasize skills stretching across everything students do. Don't always give students the answer. When asking a question they can't answer, don't immediately throw out a lifeline and ask if they need help before giving a hint or choosing others to answer the question. Let them struggle.

De-emphasize test scores, grades, and averages. This is one of the toughest things to let go of in education. Many schools still require grade point averages because it's how they rank students, and our higher education system uses GPA to determine how successful students will be in college. Educators need to completely rethink this premise. Let students retake quizzes until they are able to master the content. If you have to maintain a grade, keep the student's highest score instead of averaging the scores together. Get rid of the honor roll. Shift to standards-based grading. When students do complete an assessment, focus on feedback and reviewing mistakes rather than the final grade. Let students fix their mistakes to prove they have learned the skills and content.

Minimize the need for perfection. Show students things don't have to be flawless in order to be shared. Don't punish mistakes. Let students produce bad work in order to produce good work. Have you ever encountered students who can't start their writing until they have thought of the perfect opening sentence? The struggle for perfection hinders the process, and after thirty minutes of "writing," they haven't written a single thing. Try to get students into the habit of sharing even when they think something is less than perfect. Model this for students and encourage their process.

Mistakes can be powerful tools in your classroom when harnessed effectively. You have the ability to create a culture of mistake-making by modeling your process—warts and all. Show students you make mistakes and then learn from those mistakes: *I tried this last time, but it didn't work. Let me try it a different way!* Giving students the chance to make mistakes—and celebrating those mistakes as a means to learning and growth—encourages errors as part of the learning process. Every single person makes mistakes: teachers, students, administrators, parents. *Everyone.* Combine those mistakes and make them part of the classroom. As Groucho Marx said, "Learn from the mistakes of others. You can never live long enough to make them all yourself."

SECRET SAUCE SUMMARY

- Effective educators make many mistakes. Then they reflect upon, learn, and grow from those mistakes.

- Model the mistake-making process for students, as well as your reflection process. Let students see what it looks like to think critically about a mistake and develop a plan for moving forward.

- Admit your mistakes. Own them, and share them to help others grow. Make intentional mistakes so students know they are a part of everyday actions.

- Focus on the process and not the end product. Emphasize the learning taking place throughout your process is much more important than the final product or final grade.

Planning and Reflecting

What is the biggest mistake you ever made as an educator? How did you learn from the mistake? How did you grow as a professional educator?

_____

_____

_____

How do you encourage a mistake-making culture for students? What actions can you take to promote growth from mistakes?

_____

_____

_____

How do you model mistake-making for students? What other steps can you take to include more modeling of mistakes?

_____

_____

_____

How can you minimize the impact of grades on your students' ability to embrace mistake-making?

_____

_____

_____

Add Your Own SECRET SAUCE Ingredients

List three actions you will take to embrace the power of mistakes.

1. _____

_____

_____

2. _____

_____

_____

3. _____

_____

_____

Chapter 6

TIME

*The bad news is time flies. The good
news is you're the pilot.*

—MICHAEL ALTSHULER

What You Need to Know: Time is one of the most valuable
commodities you have as a teacher. Make sure the activities
and experiences you plan for students are valuable and provide a return on investment for the time used.

Time Wasters

As a teacher, I spent my early mornings dutifully writing the "Do
Now" on the board. The Do Now was supposed to engage students as soon as they walked in the door so they wasted no time.
Ironically, the Do Now was probably one of the biggest time wasters built into our day—a vacuum sucking time from our day and
stealing the will to live from students. Over the years, I tried to
modify it. For a while, students reviewed their math homework
collaboratively, which was fine in and of itself. Then I made the
mistake of taking an additional ten to fifteen minutes to review
certain problems with the whole class. For some reason, the

activities I utilized to start the day actually cost us more time than they saved.

Unfortunately, I never considered how valuable the activity was for students. I just knew every other teacher in my school did it; therefore, I had to do it as well. And my biggest problem was I never thought about how I was actually using my time. And when you are not thinking about how you are using your given time, it is easy to let it slip away and discover you are wasting your valuable time on unimportant things. In fact, it is much, much easier to waste time than to conserve it.

As an administrator, I've seen firsthand how time management can be a difficult skill to master. The teacher's fifteen-minute mini-lesson ballooned into a twenty-seven-minute lesson. Suddenly, the teacher realizes how much time was taken up by the lesson, apologizes to students, explains why it took so long, reiterates what students should be focusing on—the point of the mini-lesson—and then students begin their writing process. What should have been thirty minutes to write has now dwindled to ten minutes. The students begin to write, but just a few sentences in, they are given a two-minute warning to begin cleaning up to move on to the next subject area.

As a teacher, I've been in this situation. After it had happened, I sat down and tried to figure out what had happened to the time I'd been given. How did it slip away so quickly? What could I have done differently to explain the concept? How could I have taken less time during the mini-lesson? Why did students only write a few sentences? The questions went on and on until I realized I'd spent ten *more* minutes trying to figure out how I lost time in the first place! It's a vicious cycle. Once you become accustomed to wasting time, it becomes easier to waste time. You will find excuses and justifications for your time-wasting and, more importantly, students will pick up on your modeling. They will become time wasters as well!

Three Different Ways to Start Class

1. **Question Flooding.** Invite students to generate their own questions. Let them write down as many questions as they have about the day's topic or questions they still have about the previous day's lesson.

2. **Generating Solutions to Real-World Problems.** Focus on real-world problems students are dealing with. Pose the problem and let students write down as many solutions as possible. Remember, initially, no idea is a bad idea!

3. **Genius Hour.** Let students focus on something they are passionate about. Use the first five, ten, or fifteen minutes of class to allow students to research a topic and create something around the topic. It could be a TED Talk style speech about a topic, an elevator pitch or presentation for a new product they've created, or a blog or podcast about a topic they are passionate about.

I've also been in classrooms where the opposite happens. The teacher plans a forty-minute math lesson and, wanting to avoid the lesson going long, zooms through it in six minutes. Suddenly, students are completing their guided and independent practice problems just a couple of minutes later. Some students even complete the extension activity quickly. A dozen hands go up, and each student utters the same timeworn phrase: *I'm done. What should I do now?* The teacher looks up at the clock and realizes the forty-minute lesson has been completed in just eighteen minutes. Twenty-two valuable minutes still remain, but without a plan, they too will somehow be frittered away on emergency planning, apologies, and meaningless activities, wasting everyone's time—again.

Avoid the Time Sucks

You have a forty-minute planning period and a to-do list of nine items. You plan to tackle the list, and you hope to check off four or five items during your planning session. You go online to look for a lesson—and get caught up looking for easy holiday crafts your students can complete. Before you know it, the forty minutes is up, and it's time to go back to your students.

We've all been guilty of it.

Any number of activities, websites, and other leisurely experiences can suck you in. The time sucks are amazingly good at getting you to squander the extra five or ten minutes you thought you would utilize to get some tasks done. How many of these time sucks have snagged you?

Online teacher sites. You search the latest—and what you think might be the *greatest*—blogs and posts by other teachers to get ideas for your lessons and classroom, even though many of the projects and lessons are meaningless busy work that have no impact on student learning. But they look cute, so you move from one picture to the next without realizing the time you are losing. This is why lesson planning, which *could* take forty minutes, takes three hours of your weekend.

The meandering side conversation. I'm all for a good conversation, but sometimes the discussions I engage in lack productive outcomes. This is why teachers don't accomplish anything during their prep period. They get into a discussion with a colleague about the latest reality TV show, or worse, the conversation veers toward idle gossip, banter, and chatter about other coworkers and what they are—or are *not*—doing in their classrooms. At best, the meandering side conversation turns into an absolute time suck. At worst, tall tales are spread about colleagues and *will* eventually get back to them. Then you need several more conversations to repair relationships or fix a problem that had been easily avoidable in the first place.

Flat-out negativity. Complaining is super easy. Try it. Think about something making you unhappy right now. You probably just thought of at least a dozen topics sticking in your craw. You can now probably rant for the next hour about them. But I'm going to ask you to kindly refrain from doing so—in order to continue with this book! Engaging in negativity throughout your day can be one of the ultimate time sucks. You hear a colleague complaining about something, and you jump on the bandwagon. You say something in the lunchroom about a negative experience you are having, and everyone else begins to chime in with their own complaints. Before you know it, everyone leaves lunch in a bad mood due to the negative vibe *you* started. While it is much harder to remain positive throughout the day, if you do, you might be able to avoid the endless trap of time-sucking defeatism and hopelessness.

Searching for the perfect lesson. You are ready to teach the perfect lesson on westward expansion. You just need the perfect short video to launch it. You fire up YouTube and type in "westward expansion." You watch the first video, which lasts approximately six minutes. You need something a little shorter, in the three- to four-minute range. You find a westward expansion rap clocking in at three minutes forty seconds, but after you watch the video, you realize it is a little too cheesy. This goes on and on until you find the perfect video, the perfect activity, the perfect questions, *and* the perfect exit activity. By the time you're finished, you've spent ninety minutes planning one forty-five-minute lesson. Every lesson doesn't have to be perfect, and sometimes you just need to find a video to start a meaningful discussion among students. You can even start the lesson with a simple question to get students talking. Don't always hold out for perfection. Give in to the fact that not every lesson needs to be perfect, and free yourself from this time suck!

Everyone has been attacked by time sucks. They are so enticing. They draw you in, and before you know it, the time sucks will waste every extra minute you have. Be aware of the time you dedicate to these dangerous practices. Is it okay to talk to a colleague about a TV show once in a while? Absolutely! Is it okay to look online for lesson inspiration occasionally? Certainly. But be careful of the time sucks. They can take away your minutes, your hours, your days, and even your weekends!

Make the Most of Your Time

Time will never be on your side. No matter how much you try to squeeze into the day or rearrange your schedule, time is too valuable to waste on unimportant activities. How then do we take advantage of the time we are given?

Use a time inventory. Start by completing a time inventory to find out how you spend your daily time allotment. If your school is like most, you may have a six-plus-hour day, or a forty- or forty-five-minute period with students. Follow the steps below to complete your inventory and evaluate how you use your time.

- *Write down what you do with your time.* You probably spend fifteen to twenty minutes eating lunch, but what does the rest of your day look like? What activities are you focusing on? Do you spend five to ten minutes taking attendance at the beginning of a period or the beginning of the day? Do you check homework with the whole class even though 95 percent of the students understood it?
- *Allocate your time.* Once you have a list of all of the things you do in a day, write down the number of minutes used to complete each item.

- *Begin a deep analysis of your schedule.* What are the non-negotiables? What activities have the most impact on student learning? These are the activities that you will not remove from your schedule. Star those on your list and retain them.
- *Prioritize activities.* Look at the activities that are most helpful to students if done the right way. Put a plus sign next to these activities. Continue to do these activities as long as they are implemented properly and don't become a waste of precious time.
- *Cross out.* Finally, look at the tasks you are only doing because everyone else is doing them or they have been a traditional part of how you run your classroom. Ask yourself a simple question: *Is this meaningful?* If you find an activity adds value, keep it. If it does not add value, cross it out and never do it again.

Take things off the table. There are only so many hours in the day, and even fewer hours in the school day. After you complete your time inventory, the most difficult task will be cutting things out. Some necessary tasks and activities will need to be eliminated to fit into the day. Most schools use between 240 and 300 instructional minutes per day, and wasting any of these precious minutes can deter from what you are trying to accomplish. Deciding what to eliminate will be the problem. Some activities will suck you in with nostalgia: *We've always done this. I know it's not in our curriculum, but the kids love it, and it's always been something the second grade does!* Some things may look good on paper but not actually work when implemented in the classroom. (I'm talking to you, Do Now!) If an action or activity doesn't add value, it's got to go. Sometimes the hardest part is saying goodbye!

Be prepared to take things off the table in order to add things to the table. This is the key to a time inventory. Activities on the list with a plus sign next to them are tasks and exercises that might be worthwhile for students. At one time, teachers were asked to commit daily minutes to timed "fact tests" in math. By completing a time inventory, you might decide this is not the best use of time for *all* students. You may stumble across something more beneficial, or you may be required to add something by an administrator or the state. If you question the value of an activity or if it's not done well, it might be one of the first things to go in order to make room for something else.

Have a meaningful plan, a backup plan, and a backup for the backup! First and foremost, know exactly how you plan to use your time. As a new teacher, I planned everything down to the minute. My lessons didn't always follow my carefully detailed timeline, but I had a sense of where we were going at all times. It took several years before I could move away from the minute-by-minute agenda. When I did, it was almost freeing. I would list our goals, along with several other objectives we could attack if we had time or if there was a change in plans. The backup list proved to be a lifesaver for me and my students. As we got better at time management, we were able to move from one activity to the next without wasting time deciding what to do next. Start here with A, then move on to B, then C. If you can't start with A, then jump right into B and C. Students knew the backup list as well as I did and were ready to move on when something interrupted their initial plan.

Five Ways to End a Class or End the Day

1. **Reflect. Review. To do.** Take a few minutes at the end of the day to complete this three-part activity. Ask students to *reflect* on their learning for the day, *review* what they accomplished during the day, and complete their *to-do* list for the next day. This short exercise gives students a chance to contemplate their own learning, as well as have an action plan for how to continue their learning. Plus, the to-do list can help students practice organization and planning skills!

2. **Read.** Spending time in classrooms reading for pure joy is not done enough. One of my favorite times to visit classrooms is just after lunch, when students and teachers return to the classroom, pick up their favorite books, find a comfy spot, and read. Teachers model the *joy* of reading, and I usually talk to students about the books they are reading. This is also a great strategy for ending the day or finishing up a class period. It can provide a calm, peaceful sign-off to the day.

3. **Appreciation, apology, aha.** Circle up students at the conclusion of your day, giving each student the opportunity to share an *appreciation* for someone or something, an *apology* to someone, or an *"aha"* moment of realization. This sixty-second strategy was created by Aukeem Ballard of Summit Public Schools in Redwood City, California (edutopia.org/video/60-second-strategy-appreciation-apology-aha), and it allows you to further build community, restore relationships when necessary, and share in the light bulb moments taking place. Our staff has even finished our staff meetings with this activity, and everyone always goes home on a positive note.

4. Brain dump. Ever have a fleeting idea or spark of recognition about something and then fail to remember it just a few minutes later? The brain dump can be a powerful tool to get students engaging in metacognition—thinking about their own *thinking*. It's simple. Have students write down (Yay, analog!) or type up (Yay, digital!) their thoughts for five minutes at the end of a session. This is completely informal writing with no focus on grammar or structure—literally just putting words down. It could be a sketchnote, bullet points, or just words. No thought is bad. Everything gets written down. Students may have questions about the day's learning or write about a new understanding of a concept. They may have an idea for a project they want to start or a story in their head needing to get out. Once or twice a week, ask students to read over their brain dump notes. It may help them be more conscious of how they think about a topic, or it may spark an idea igniting them to start creating. Either way it can be a valuable tool to inspire students.

5. A moment of clarity. Occasionally, everyone needs a moment just to breathe. One of my favorite times for this is on Friday afternoons after everyone has left the building. I sit at my desk and attempt to clear my mind. After a few deep breaths, I try to focus on *nothing*. It can sometimes be difficult, but I always feel better when I do it. Give students a moment of clarity to finish their day, too. Take a minute or two and have students engage in a deep-breathing exercise. Then guide them to clear their minds. It can be a relaxing way to end the hustle and bustle of your daily school lives.

Schedules do not need to be wholesale. Schools are well beyond the days of all the desks in rows facing the front of the classroom (more on this later!) with all students working on the same worksheet at the same time. In this regard, schedules don't have to be the same across the board. A valuable activity for one student may be a complete waste of time for another. Think about the student who already started kindergarten as a reader and knows her sight words. Other students will benefit from learning letters, but her spending time on this task would be a fool's errand. Plan your schedule to allow flexibility. While some students work at centers or stations to practice necessary skills, give others time to work on their writing or participate in "Maker" activities where students tinker, make, and create, or Genius Hour, where they focus on a passion project. When you are working with small groups and providing necessary interventions for struggling students, allow others to go beyond the curriculum to stretch their thinking.

Kill two birds with one stone. Because time is so valuable, find ways to plan to double up on the use of time. Think about the power of *and*. A nature walk is a great way to explore for science *and* get your students up and moving. It can also inspire students to write or create artistically. Introducing an exercise similar to speed dating around a specific topic gets students talking about content *and* practices necessary social skills *and* builds relationships *and* provides movement. Students constructing a model at the end of the week to show how they are thinking about a concept provides an opportunity for informal assessment *and* a chance for students to create. One of the solutions to your ever-growing time crunch is to make sure the activities you implement provide value. There is no better way to add value than to reach multiple goals at the same time.

Leave white space in your schedule. As contradictory as this may sound, leaving gaps of time in your daily schedule may actually help you accomplish more. White space is a visual-arts term that is often referred to as "negative space." It is the visual space on a page not covered with color or design. It can often say more than what is actually covered on the page. Fed Ex's logo is a great example.

The white space between the *E* and the *X* forms an arrow. It communicates that FedEx is always moving forward.

Sometimes the white space in your schedule can be more important than the activities. If you are an elementary teacher, leaving open a thirty-minute block at the end of your day might give some students an opportunity to finish any work they didn't finish earlier in the day, give other students the chance to get started on homework while you are there to support them, or give others an outlet and necessary time to quietly read or draw. At the secondary level, using five to ten minutes at the end of a period—or block schedule—or using an entire period at the end of the week can accomplish these same things for middle and high school students. Recognize that things always come up: fire drills or the unexpected assembly you forgot to write on your calendar and only remembered when your principal called your room and asked, "Is your class joining us for the assembly?" (Unfortunately, I've done this to teachers. Not my best moments!)

If you jam-pack your schedule, accounting for every minute and every second, you and your students will only find yourselves frustrated, stressed, and angry when these emergencies or scheduling snafus arise. But if you leave small gaps of white space within your daily schedule, you can easily overcome these obstacles, or provide students with a moment to reflect or just breathe. The white space can often be a welcome respite within your overbooked days!

Time, regrettably, will never be on your side. You will always be at its mercy. Your goal should be to work within the constraints of bell schedules and instructional minute allotments to find value and meaningful work. Determine how you are *really* using your allotted time. Analyze it on a deeper level. Try to eliminate the practices simply wasting time. Allow yourself a moment to breathe. The key is to think *actively* about how you use your time. If you don't, you will frivolously fritter it away.

SECRET SAUCE SUMMARY

- Since your days include very few hours, make sure you fill them with meaningful activities and experiences providing value.

- Complete a time inventory to analyze how you and your students spend each minute of your day.

- Take things off the table. If you find you are doing some things that don't provide any real value, get rid of them.

- Be prepared *within* your schedule. Have a backup plan, and let students know what it is. This way, if something goes wrong, everyone has a plan to fall back on so time is not wasted.

- Design your schedule with flexibility in mind so students can accomplish a variety of individual tasks. The schedule should be open enough to have multiple groups of students working on different activities if necessary.

- Plan your schedule so you can accomplish multiple outcomes at the same time. Relish the power of *and*.

- Leave white space within your schedule. Build in open blocks of time to accomplish the things you never got to or to handle those emergencies arising throughout the day.

Planning and Reflecting

What are the most meaningful experiences within your schedule providing real value for you and students? What are the activities or tasks providing the least value for you and students?

_____

_____

_____

_____

What actions or exercises can you legitimately cross off your list? What are the ones you can get rid of?

_____

_____

_____

What kind of *two birds, one stone* activities would make a more efficient use of time for you and students?

_____

_____

_____

How would you ultimately like to use your time? If you had extra time, what types of experiences would you like to have? Where can you find time to actually fit them into your schedule?

_____

_____

_____

How can you improve your use of allotted time? How can you limit time-wasting actions?

_____

_____

_____

Add Your Own SECRET SAUCE Ingredients

List three actions you will take to better use your time.

1. _____

_____

_____

2. _____

_____

_____

3. _____

_____

_____

A Recipe for Success

Effective Lessons

As I prepared to write this section, I asked myself a simple question: *what are the most effective lessons I've ever taught?*

First, I had to define the word *effective*. Did it mean students were engaged? Or students understood the content when I assessed them? Did it mean I was meeting the learning objective in a short amount of time? Ultimately, I settled on this definition: "effective" means students would remember the learning objective years after they had left me, and they would carry the knowledge they had gained with them forever.

So which of my lessons were most effective? Several popped into my mind. I facilitated a Socratic discussion among my fifth-grade students on social justice and the civil rights movement during a social studies lesson. The discussion was uncomfortable because students asked difficult questions, but students left the two-day discussion with a better understanding of social justice. They internalized it, and for the rest of the year, their behaviors and actions changed.

Was my most effective lesson our study of plants when I let students list any questions they had and then provided support as they decided how to share what they learned with classmates? Some groups created slide presentations and some gave oral reports. One group dressed up my friend Nick (from chapter two) as a flower, complete with brown sweatpants to represent his roots, a green shirt to represent his stem, and a mask labeled with the other parts of the flower. He stood in the front of the class to *teach* and *entertain*. Nick's group showed the class how shade and lack of light could impact the growth of a flower, with Nick pantomiming one of the most Oscar-worthy death scenes I've ever seen a student acting like a flower participate in! We *all* learned from this lesson.

Could my most effective lesson be the math lesson where a student taught his own method for long division? Students had the opportunity to learn "the Keville Method for Long Division" from a classmate who saw numbers in a different way. (Thanks to Michael Keville for his outside of the box thinking!) Several students within the class found the alternative method easier than traditional long division, and the fact that a classmate showed them rather than me showing them ensured they would continue to use this approach long after they left my classroom.

As I thought about the many lessons I taught over the years—the good, the bad, and the ugly—I realized the most effective lessons all had one thing in common: they were all driven by students. If you want to use an educational buzzword to describe these lessons, you would call them "student-centered." Students were able to internalize and own their learning because they were actively involved in creating the lessons. When students own their learning in this way, they are able to maintain the knowledge base well beyond a chapter or unit test, even well beyond the class. Because they guided the learning process, the learning belongs to them forever.

The following are some strategies you can utilize to make your lessons more effective.

Establish purpose and expected learning outcomes. When designing a learning experience for students, you need to consider a few things to guarantee the activity has the impact you seek. Ask yourself four simple questions to ensure you are getting to the heart of the experience:

- *What is the purpose of the experience?* Determine what you want students to learn and know your *why*. Why is this learning important, and how will it help students? If your *why* is relevant and meaningful, you can respond to the age-old question, "When will I ever use this in life?" Better yet, you will not get the question at all because students will immediately see the relevance.

- *Why does it matter to students?* This is where the relationships you build with students will come into play. Knowing the students' *why*s is just as important as knowing your own. Why is it important to them? If you can help them see why a learning experience is paramount to their lives, they have a much better chance of owning their learning.

- *How will students be able to employ their own learning strategies?* This one is rather simple. Are you building opportunities for student *voice* and *choice* into the lesson or unit of study? If so, students will be able to make the content more relevant for their own purposes.

- *What are the expected learning outcomes?* Determine what you want students to learn or do based on the learning experience. Are they consuming content, creating content, or connecting content? Knowing the learning outcome can help you plan a more meaningful learning experience for students. In fact, starting from the expected outcome and working backward can often help you better design lesson activities to meet the outcome.

Remember the importance of planning and preparation. When great instruction is happening in your classroom, you often don't think of the time, effort, and planning involved in making the lesson successful. It's important to ensure you have preplanned a number of key factors in order to ensure its success.

- *Script ten questions you'd like to ask during a lesson.* One of the most difficult skills to master as a teacher is questioning. Asking a great, higher-order thinking question is hard in the moment. If you write down the ten questions you definitely want to ask, you will have a much better chance of actually asking these questions. Having the questions prepared lets you focus on other aspects of your lesson without having to think of good questions on the fly.

- *Prepare activities to engage learners who meet the lesson objective quickly.* Face it. You will prepare the greatest of lessons for your students, and one student—or a small group of students—will already know what you are trying to teach. Some students who enter your classroom with previous knowledge about the content will be ready to move on from your forty-minute lesson in just six minutes. How will those students continue learning? Extension activities can be a lifesaver. Spending time up front to prepare meaningful activities—not just busywork!—can help extend learning for students. Don't make the mistake of penalizing fast learners with worksheets or busywork. If students finish early, find a meaningful activity to stretch their thinking. Genius Hour is a great way to engage students who are fast finishers.

- *Consider what steps you will take for students who don't get it the first time.* Along with the group of students who are ready to move on quickly, you will also have a group of students who struggle to pick up a concept. You need to consider what steps to take in order to help those having difficulty, as well. Prepare a few strategies or reteaching methods you can utilize at the first sign of struggle for students. This will allow you to take action immediately rather than having to figure out how to tackle it on the fly.

- *Carefully plan your student partnerships prior to the lesson.* Whenever you are planning collaborative work in the classroom, contemplate the strengths and needs of individual students and how they might work with other students. Keep in mind some students might work better individually than they will in certain partnerships. Don't just leave student groups and partnerships up to chance. Give students the best chance to be successful by considering who works well together.

- *Always have a backup plan!* Even with the best-laid plans, in order, something usually goes awry. Have an alternative plan ready to save the day. Technology not working for you? Make sure you have a plan for students to complete some substantial work without their computers or have students utilize their own backup devices. Did a fire drill interrupt your most important lesson of the year? Be able to modify the forty-five-minute lesson down to a twenty-five-minute lesson so essential learning still takes place.

Assessment is NOT just a test. Making sure you assess a student does not mean simply having them complete a quiz or test at the end of a chapter. Assessment should occur in a variety of formats and be ongoing throughout the learning process, not just a summative determination of what a student knows on a certain date. Carefully consider exactly how you are assessing students in your classroom.

- *Have an assortment of assessments.* No single measure should be used to determine how a student is learning. Use a combination of summative and formative assessments to figure out exactly where students are in their learning process. Observe, take anecdotal notes, and provide specific feedback to help guide students. Try to include a variety of formative assessments each day to help students reflect on their own learning. Consider using some of the following methods.
  - **Three questions.** Students write down three questions summarizing what they have learned during

the day. Ask them to share the questions with a partner when finished to see if they can answer each other's questions.

- **Do and don't.** Students fold a paper in half to create two columns: "Do" and "Don't." Using the columns, students share information about what they learned. This quick, formative assessment works particularly well for math. For example, Do: Line up numbers according to place value when doing multi-digit addition or subtraction. Don't: Forget to check the operation when completing multi-digit addition or subtraction.

- **Tweet it out.** Have students share what they learned in 280 characters or less. Combine this with an actual class Twitter account and ask students to share their learning with the world. After each student writes their "tweet of the day," pick one to go live on your class feed.

- **One-minute video.** Let students record a one-minute video reflection to share their learning for the day. They can record using a personal device or use a technology tool like Flipgrid to make the reflection quick and easy!

- **Three, two, one.** At the end of class, ask students to list *three* things to remember, *two* things they enjoyed learning about, and *one* question they still have. Use the questions to guide students and provide feedback.

- **PMI.** Students can examine an idea from different viewpoints by listing a *Plus*, a *Minus*, and something *Interesting*. When students think about a concept from multiple perspectives, they can begin to develop a more concrete understanding of the concept.

- *Use assessment to guide instruction.* Many assumed data would help revolutionize education. With multiple data points on each student, teachers would be able to provide individualized instruction to every student, reaching them through their own interests at their own academic levels. Instead, educators have been on a wild-goose chase to collect data, and once they have all sorts of data on students, they are paralyzed and inundated by it. Keep it simple. Gather basic data from assessments and use it to plan and guide instruction. Use an exit ticket to see how well students understood linear equations. After reviewing the exit tickets, plan small groups for the next day's lesson. Some students will need additional support; some will extend their learning beyond the basic concept.

- *Know a student's assessment strengths and weaknesses.* Some students perform really well on standardized tests; others do not. A student may struggle with testing anxiety when asked to perform on a test or in a timed setting. Keep in mind every assessment does not work for every student. A student may understand a concept but not be able to convey the understanding based on the type of assessment. Does a student perform better when asked to share verbally? Give them this opportunity and assess them by asking questions about what they learned. Does a student perform particularly well when drawing a picture of what they learned? Let the student share a sketchnote to demonstrate what they know.

Chapter 7

SUPPORT

There is nothing more beautiful than someone who goes out of their way to make life beautiful for others.

—MANDY HALE

What You Need to Know: Students come to you with a variety of strengths and needs. It is of the utmost importance to provide students with the support they need to be successful in your classroom.

Every Child Is Different

Every child who walks through your door will have different needs. Some will be easy to meet; some will not. Some will be extreme, and you will need significant help to provide support for these students. But in order for every student to learn and achieve his or her best, you must provide that support. Some will ask, "If I provide extra support for this one child, is it fair to the other children in the class?" The answer is an emphatic *absolutely!* Everyone has different strengths and needs; providing individual support means you are doing exactly what each child needs in order to learn. It might be different from what another child is getting, but it is undoubtedly necessary and appropriate.

Just recently, our school established a sensory area in our main office because we have many students who require sensory input in order to stay focused throughout the day. We included a sensory walk area where students walk, tip-toe, jump, hop, and spin their way through a short course. After they complete the walk, the students set a timer for three minutes and are allowed to play with any number of sensory tools for a brief time. Building bricks, magnetic toys, connecting blocks, and fidgets allow students to get some sensory stimulation.

We placed the sensory area in our main office due to a lack of space and to ensure students would be supervised while using it. Initially, we had concerns about how the use of the sensory area would impact the normal functioning of the main office. We wondered if students would take advantage of this opportunity and spend more time there than necessary or if they would be a distraction to staff members trying to use the office. Ultimately, we realized the walk to the office, sensory input, and brain break were exactly what some students needed in order to refocus once they returned to their classroom.

Our entire staff realizes we are supporting students in what they need, and it benefits all of us for students to be more focused so they can learn better. Some students use the sensory area on an as-needed basis, maybe visiting once a day or once a week. Some students have never used the sensory area because they don't require it. A couple of students have regularly scheduled sensory breaks throughout their day, visiting the office as many as five times each day. What we have learned throughout our implementation is that we have to find the right balance for each student. We have to make sure we are giving the *individual* student exactly what he or she needs.

Provide Better Support

In order to provide better support for each of your individual students, consider the following:

Individual feedback is important. One of the most impactful actions you can take in the classroom is to provide timely feedback to individual students. If students are working on a piece of writing, specific feedback can help students move forward. Avoid the generic and bland "great job" or "needs more." Provide specific, purposeful suggestions like, "Think about including a stronger lead to hook the reader. Try to brainstorm some other leads."

The feedback doesn't always have to come from you. In fact, it might be more powerful when it comes from a peer. Students who can learn to provide specific feedback to classmates are internalizing the learning process and communicating ways to improve. Those sharing feedback are also learning in the process. Teach and model opportunities to provide constructive criticism or involve students in the feedback loop.

The following are some specific feedback strategies you may want to try:

- *I notice and I wonder.* Give students the opportunity to observe the work of other students and then provide feedback by sharing two sticky notes with their classmates. The *I Noticed* note includes something the student did particularly well. The *I Wonder* note asks about something the student may not have considered or included. You can also structure this as *One (Thing) to Praise and One (Thing) to Grow On.*
- *The feedback stream.* Pixar has made some of the greatest animated movies of all time by incorporating feedback meetings into its creative process. While a movie is being made, the entire team will gather to analyze and provide

feedback on each scene. Use this model to provide a feedback stream for your students. Ask a student to share his or her writing or thinking, and allow the entire class to add "notes" for the student to consider. The key is making sure you model what productive feedback looks like. Suggestions should be specific and seek to move students forward in their thinking.

You may need to adjust your pace or timing. Not every student will learn at the same pace. When a baby is first learning to walk, his parents don't stop when he is ten months old and say, "Our child hasn't walked yet. He is a failed walker!" They provide support. Babies use "walkers" to help support them—literally—as they learn to walk, and one of the most important types of support parents can provide is the gift of time. Some babies will walk as early as nine months, while others might take twelve months. Some may even take sixteen or seventeen months to begin walking. The same goes for the skills students are learning in your classroom. Some may arrive in fourth grade already understanding long division, some may pick up the skill in a few weeks, and some may take a month or more. You need to exercise patience in your expectations for students. As with parents and their children, one of the best supports you can provide for students is the gift of time. Let students work at their own paces. Don't provide artificial time limits and constraints; it could possibly stifle your students' learning process.

Consider replacing your time limits and schedule deadlines with time and schedule *guidelines* instead. Some students may need extended time to finish an activity or project, and this is okay. Limiting the amount of time and holding to an arbitrary timeline might negatively impact the learning process of your students. Consider adding the word *about* to provide more flexibility for students: "This project will be due in *about* two weeks."

Everyone can benefit from modifications or accommodations. In every school, we recognize modifications and accommodations are part of Individualized Education Plans for students with special education needs, as well as 504 plans for students with specialized learning needs. By law, we need to modify learning for these students or provide special accommodations to help these students learn. Many educators have realized, though, that making modifications or accommodations can help *all* students. Providing a note-taking graphic organizer can benefit all students, not just one who needs help with organization. Placing fewer questions on a page and providing more white space can help all students. Taking frequent breaks can help all students.

Try implementing these universal accommodations to benefit all students in your class:

- *Provide built-in breaks.* If you work with younger students, you know—or will soon learn—movement breaks can do wonders for increasing focus and productivity. The same is true for older students. Build in a mid-class "stand and stretch" break. Play a popular song and institute a dance break halfway through class. Schedule breaks throughout your day so students can refocus and reenergize.
- *Directions should be both written and verbal.* All students will benefit from hearing *and* seeing directions. Write your directions on the board, and students can reference them if they forget halfway through an assignment. Provide a detailed list of assignment tasks, and read through the list aloud with students. The sharing of directions both verbally and in written form will mean you have fewer students asking, "Wait, what are we supposed to do again?"
- *Increase wait or processing time.* This is an easy implementation benefiting every one of your students. When asking a student a question, increase the wait time before you try

to prompt him or her, or before offering help from another student. Many teachers will wait somewhere between three and five seconds, but some students may need as many as ten seconds to process the question. Increase wait time to as much as seven seconds per question, or better yet, let students pair with partners to share their answers before asking anyone to share with the larger group.

Scaffold tasks and projects. When you say to students, "Please read this ten-page article and answer these five reflection questions. The assignment will be due on Wednesday," you might be unintentionally setting up some students for failure. The key to scaffolding is providing tools or structures to allow students to move from intentional support to independence while still completing the tasks at their own comfort levels. The beautiful thing about scaffolds is students can work within the structures provided by you to complete the task on their own, at their own pace and comfort level. Consider using some of the following scaffolding techniques with your students.

- *Break assignments into chunks.* When assigning a project stretching through several tasks and activities, be sure to break the assignment into chunks. It's much easier for students to complete seven manageable chunks than to complete one massive project they might initially see as overwhelming and impossible to finish. Break apart each task and provide guidelines for completion: *First, you will need to visit this website to research information. After you complete this, record notes from your research before moving on to step three.* Giving students a guideline can help them be more successful.
- *Give students context by pre-teaching vocabulary.* Based on their life experience, some students might be at a disadvantage when it comes to their vocabulary. With any new

content students might be learning, pre-teach vocabulary so students have a context when they see a new word in print. Provide the definitions of unknown words prior to a lesson or have students preview an article you will ask them to read and identify words they may not be familiar with. Then ask students to work in pairs to define those words and use them in context. Working through the article this way will help them develop a deeper understanding.

- *Provide a visual.* Every student can benefit from seeing a visual representation accompanying text information or along with a verbal description. A simple picture along with the daily schedule, for example, can help kindergarten students who might not be able to read yet. Photographs accompanying your lecture on a specific topic may help solidify an idea in your students' minds. A graphic organizer can help students organize information in a visual manner, making it more memorable.

Give students exactly what they need. The question I most often hear from educators in regard to providing support is, "If I do this for one student, don't I have to do it for *all* students?" And the simple answer is *No.* Don't be afraid to differentiate or personalize learning for individual students. While some accommodations may help all students, some will need to be made only for specific children. Students may have a medical situation necessitating a personalized option, or they may require a unique academic support. Give it to them. Provide every student with exactly what he or she requires in order to be successful in your classroom. The ideas below may help you give your students exactly what they need.

- *Set personal learning plans for each student.* Start the school year by establishing a few goals with each student, along with the type of support each will need from you.

This personal learning plan will be fluid throughout the year but should provide a basic outline of how you can best support each individual learner.

- *Offer additional learning pathways.* Traditionally, there was just one pathway to learning: *the goal is to learn X by following process A.* With the advent of advanced technology, educators can now say, "Our goals are to learn X, Y, and Z by following processes A, B, C, D, E, and F. If these processes don't work for you, there are twenty more letters in the alphabet!" Teachers can now show students multiple ways to learn something.

In chapter two, I talked about the importance of establishing high expectations for students. As an educator, you can have the absolute highest expectations for students, but they can still fail to meet the expectations because you don't provide the support they need to meet them. Providing *strong support* for *all* students is one of the only ways to help them meet your expectations. Individual support allows every student to learn at a high level, regardless of his or her starting point. The structures and tools you provide allow students to feel completely supported in your classroom. Make sure the support you provide can benefit each and every student in his or her own learning process.

Five Ideas for Student Reflection

Providing students with time for reflection at the end of a lesson can help them internalize information or solidify their learning process. Try these strategies for getting students to reflect on their own learning:

1. **Use an online survey tool**. Use a tool like Google Forms or SurveyMonkey to quickly gather assessment data from students. Create a Google Form for students to complete at the end of class. Once you have the results, use them to plan future instructional goals and lessons.

2. **Utilize video reflections**. Students can often have difficulty writing about what they have learned, so why not let them record a video of themselves *talking* about what they have learned? Students can quickly record themselves using any device to share their learning. To make it truly meaningful, record a video yourself and share some video feedback to students.

3. **Try sketchnotes**. Writing down their thoughts about a lesson in a visual format can help students better remember and process information. Let students jot their notes and provide visual reminders using this extremely fun format.

4. **Assign a one-minute "paper."** Give students exactly one minute to write a "paper" describing what they learned. No formalities—students simply write down everything coming to mind as they reflect on what they learned.

5. **Differentiate reflections**. The best way to get students to reflect meaningfully on their learning is to

let them decide how they want to reflect. Give students the option to use any one of these methods, or choose one of their own, to reflect in a way most comfortable to them.

SECRET SAUCE SUMMARY

Because students enter your classroom at varying levels, with a variety of strengths and needs, you will need to provide them with individual and group supports to ensure reinforcement of learning.

- Timely and specific feedback provided by the teacher or peers will help students move forward as learners.
- Consider the pace at which students are working. You may need to slow down or speed up for certain students. Utilize flexible time guidelines instead of hard-and-fast deadlines and time limits.
- Provide modifications and accommodations appropriate for *all* learners. Some learning strategies will benefit each learner in your class.
- Supply students with scaffolding structures and tools to make tasks and assignments more manageable.
- Give students exactly what they need in order to make learning most successful for each individual student.

Planning and Reflecting

How do you support individual students within your classroom?

_____

_____

_____

Do you employ universal modifications and accommodations for _all_ students? If so, what kinds? If not, which ones can you begin to employ for all students?

_____

_____

_____

How can you provide students with additional time to master content if they require it?

_____

_____

_____

How do you provide specific and timely feedback to students? Do you allow for peer feedback? How?

_____

_____

_____

Add Your Own SECRET SAUCE Ingredients

List three actions you will take to provide better support for students.

1. _____

_____

_____

2. _____

_____

_____

3. _____

_____

_____

A Recipe for Success

Student Discipline

I've seen it done a million times, and each time I cringe. I worry about how the student feels in the moment. What was so egregious to warrant a teacher calling out a student in front of his or her peers?

Some teachers make public shaming as simple as writing a student's name on the board when she breaks a rule. Some have elaborate clip or card systems where the student actually has to move their clip and publicly shame himself. I've seen substitute teachers do it as a quick means to maintain order for a single day when they don't even know the students. I've seen new teachers who learned the method from their cooperating teacher and continue to use it because they don't know any other way to approach student discipline. I've seen twenty-year veterans who have been using the method for many years. I often wonder how many kids left their classrooms with a negative feeling after being called out in front of their peers?

In many cases, publicly calling a student out may stop the offending behavior. This is done through embarrassing a student, however, something we should *never* do. In some cases, trying to embarrass a student will escalate the situation quickly. Some students will react to public shaming by trying to win the interaction. All too often, I've seen it go down a terrible path for both the student and the teacher.

> Teacher: Alex, I see you are speaking when I am trying to speak. Please write your name on the board.
>
> Student: [Sits silently without moving.]

Teacher: [More agitated.] I've asked you to write your name on the board. Please do so immediately.

Student: [Sheepishly.] I don't want to write my name on the board.

Teacher: [Increasing in volume and tone.] You will write your name on the board immediately or you will be sent to the principal's office.

Student: [Repeats.] I don't want to write my name on the board.

Teacher: GO TO THE OFFICE IMMEDIATELY!!!

In a matter of two minutes, the teacher has completely derailed the lesson, set a precedent for control and compliance as being the most important thing, and negatively impacted a relationship with a student. While both the teacher and student were trying to win this interaction, there is certainly no winner. And many teachers get into these battles on a daily basis, needing to prove authority and show the student who's "boss." This never works. The teacher may gain compliance for the moment, but he surely hasn't earned any respect, and he definitely has not improved the relationship with the student—all because a student was talking. When student discipline interactions ramp up from zero to sixty like this, they are damaging for everyone involved, including the rest of the students whose abilities to learn have been negatively impacted.

Earlier I talked a great deal about how building relationships with your students trumps everything else. Building those relationships can be your best preventative measure to deal with discipline. If you have established a strong, supportive classroom environment and culture where you know your students, you can often avoid getting into these battles, but there will be occasions when a student makes a poor decision and you will need to employ some type of discipline. Two students fight on the playground during a basketball game. Three students decide to use derogatory language toward a classmate at lunch. A student sends a mean message about a classmate, and it spreads to the rest of the class. There should be consequences for all of these behaviors, and it's important students understand what the limits are for inappropriate behavior. But what should the consequences be?

Here's an example of consequences you might see posted in a classroom:

If You Choose to Break a Rule:

First Time: Name written on board. Warning.

Second Time: ✓ Added to name. 15 minutes after school on Wednesday.

Third Time: ✓✓ 30 minutes after school on Wednesday

Fourth Time: ✓✓✓ 45 minutes after school on Wednesday. Parents will be notified.

Fifth Time: ✓✓✓✓ 60 minutes after school on Wednesday. Student will be sent to the Office.

Each student will start fresh on Thursday morning.

If I saw this in a classroom, I would ask several questions:

- If a student breaks a rule on a Friday, would the teacher wait a full five days before enforcing a consequence?
- If I were a student's parent, would I find out about my child's behavior only after the fourth instance?
- Doesn't every child deserve a fresh start *each* day?
- Does the additional fifteen minutes of after-school detention address the root cause of the problem behavior when the student keeps doing it?

So many justifiable questions exist, and yet so many classrooms still operate within this sort of compliance culture.

Instead of the compliance culture of consequences, your students—and you—might be much better served by implementing a discipline system based on mutual respect, logical consequences, and addressing the underlying causes of inappropriate behaviors.

Treat students with respect and not anger. According to Benjamin Franklin, "A spoonful of honey will catch more flies than a gallon of vinegar." This holds true when you interact with a student in a disciplinary situation. Becoming angry, yelling, or trying to one-up the student during the interaction does not help the situation. In most cases, a student made a poor decision, and it wasn't meant to be a personal affront to you. By treating the student respectfully, you can have a meaningful conversation about the behavior in question and move forward. Respect students by having a private conversation with them and not resorting to public shaming. Respect them by speaking in a normal tone—not raising your voice. Respect students by remaining calm and not getting angry or trying to prove your authority.

Institute timely and logical consequences. In many instances, consequences having no connection to the problematic behavior are handed down to students. If a student uses derogatory language toward a classmate on the bus, for example, they are then required to sit out of recess. A student breaks the dress code on Monday and must serve an after-school detention on Thursday. Consequences usually have more of an impact when they are directly related to a behavior. Was a student throwing food in the cafeteria? Talk to them about who has to clean up the mess in the cafeteria and have them assist a custodian in cleaning up the tables or floors. Also, make sure consequences are timely. A disciplinary action instituted a week later may lose impact when a student doesn't even remember what he or she did wrong in the first place.

Get to the heart of the problem. Usually there is an underlying cause to many students' behavioral problems. Find out what the underlying cause is and focus on it. Addressing the root cause of a problem will help negate repeated behaviors and limit the need for further consequences. Ready to drop the hammer on the student who keeps falling asleep in your second-period class? First, find out why the child is falling asleep. Your reaction may change when you find out the child has not been getting regular sleep because his or her parents are going through an ugly divorce, yelling at each other so much the police had to be called to the house at 2:00 a.m. Knowing this information may change the consequence you want to put in place. Is a student suddenly lashing out at teachers and classmates? Finding out what's behind the sudden change in behavior may help you better address it.

Believe in fresh starts. When you hold a past behavior over a student's head, you weaken your relationship with him or her. Students need to know they will get a fresh start at all times. Being able to separate the person from the behaviors can help you provide a new beginning for students. Keep in mind, students usually do not intend to personally attack or offend you. Give them an opportunity to prove themselves. Forgive past transgressions, as long as students work to rebuild and mend relationships and restore any damage they may have caused leading to the inappropriate behavior.

Help students to restore. If a student's behavior has negatively impacted someone else, help him or her restore the relationship. Did a student yell at a classmate and call her a mean name? Help her to realize an apology might be necessary and attempt to guide the student toward rebuilding the relationship. Did a student take something from another and break it? While it might be necessary to restore the relationship, it is a *must* that the student restore the damage to the property by replacing the broken item. Helping a student reconcile with the community at large after a transgression can help the overall culture of your classroom and help maintain a positive climate with your community of learners.

Chapter 8

AUTHENTIC LEARNING OPPORTUNITIES

Content without purpose is only trivia.

—STEVE REVINGTON

What You Need to Know: Students are more engaged when their learning has meaning and purpose. Help your students find an authentic audience by connecting them to real-world problems and real-world audiences.

S top for a moment and think about your own school experience. What do you remember about school? Chances are it's not page seventy-six from your math textbook or those science definitions from chapter three. Chances are you remember the real-life opportunities you had in school to apply your learning. My school memories list is short:

- the fifth grade Math-A-Thon, where we solved math problems in order to raise money for sick children;
- the time in eighth grade when my friends and I were responsible for collaboratively creating a newspaper; and

- in high school, when I took part in service learning, spending my time helping others with a few local charity organizations.

The newspaper assignment stands out most. Each student in my class was assigned to one section of the newspaper, and I was selected for the sports section. For my friends and me, this assignment was the best thing we did all year! To say I was obsessed with sports as a kid is an understatement. No matter the sport, my friends and I dove in fully, and we were equally committed to the newspaper assignment. I was well versed in sports, poring over the sports section of our daily newspaper every morning, reading through baseball box scores, checking out the latest transactions, and constantly checking standings to see how well my favorite team, the Los Angeles Dodgers, was doing. Our teacher helped us work through the writing process, and in addition, we learned about layout, design, and placement. I probably worked harder on this one project than I had on anything else in middle school. It was authentic. I lived sports every day, and it meant something to my friends and me. Because I cared about it, I was willing to learn.

I once stood in our school's main office as some of our fifth-grade students prepared to share the morning announcements. Two of our students share a sports report every Friday, highlighting our local high school teams, noting team performances, and recognizing individuals as "players of the week." These two boys aspire to be high school athletes, and their enthusiasm was evident in the work they did each week as they engaged in this part of their learning. They loved talking about sports; therefore, they worked really hard to write their sports report each week. As I stood there, I could see myself in them. I had joked with them that they should be running their own sports podcast, and as they get older, it may be a very viable option. The skills they learned would help them tremendously as students, learners, and future members of the workforce.

Authentic Learning Experiences

As a teacher, you have likely recognized how students are more willing to learn when they are engaged in projects and activities that are meaningful to them and relevant to their own lives. So how do we engage students in these authentic learning experiences? What kind of opportunities can be organized so students can *authentically* engage in learning?

Connecting, sharing, and collaborating. Connecting with people around the world is now easier than ever for students. The power of learning is no longer limited to staying inside the four walls of your classroom. Take a look at a few ways your students can connect with others outside the classroom.

- *Mystery call.* Find a class willing to connect through Google Hangouts, Skype, or some other form of technology. Each class's students take turns asking *yes* or *no* questions to try to determine where the other class is located, such as *Are you east of the Mississippi River?* and *Is your climate mostly warm?* The first class to correctly guess where the other class lives wins the game; however, both classes truly win in terms of connecting, thinking critically, sharing, and learning with their new friends from another setting.

- *Pen pals.* While this is not exactly a new experience in education—I can remember having pen pals when I was in the third grade!—the excitement derived from the activity can lead to not only great fun but also tremendous learning. Connect students with another group of students from across the world, and have them write traditional handwritten letters or go digital using a simple tool like e-mail.

- *Shared classroom activities.* Whether students are solving a math problem, answering geography questions, or discussing the latest young adult literature, they always have more fun when they share it with others. You might find that if you connect your students with other students—a group of kids down the hall, across town, or around the world—the students who are not normally engaged tend to speak up, share, and even lead the way when other learners are involved. I've seen it happen!

I recently had the opportunity to watch fifth-grade students join their kindergarten "buddies" for a shared Genius Hour. These were students from the same building who don't often get to work together. The kindergarten teacher polled her students on what they wanted to learn. The fifth-grade teacher assigned each student one of the topics, and they were off! When I walked into the room, students were sprawled all over the classroom, learning about cooking, baseball, the circus, even nail design. The teachers could have walked out of the classroom at any time, and the students would have remained engaged. Pairing your students with others can have the same impact. Find another class and start today!

Solving real problems. School has always been separated from the real world. Students are tasked with answering made-up math questions and responding to fictitious writing prompts when plenty of real-world problems need to be solved. There is a disconnect when students spend hours a day in school disengaged, and then they go home each night to focus on what really matters to them. The best solution is to let students tackle the real world from their place in your classroom.

- *Community-based problems.* People and organizations in your community already need your students' help; plenty of real-world issues exist without having to make them up. Many high schools, for instance, have partnered with community organizations to have students build prosthetics for children in need. I have personally watched as third- and fourth-grade students in my district partnered with students in India to build solar-powered light sources and send them to those students' villages, which were in need. Seeing the impact their work could have was a powerful experience for our students.

- *School-based needs.* While global projects and problems are great for students to participate in tackling, local projects and problems also need to be addressed. At my school this year, we are hoping to involve our students in the planning and designing of an outdoor classroom space to be used by our teachers, students, and families. This type of engagement provides students with the opportunity for *voice* but also allows for many chances to incorporate learning standards surrounding research and reading, planning and writing, math and building. You can be sure students will remember these kinds of lessons more than they would any word problem they solved on page seventy-six. Find those school community members in need, and connect them with your best and brightest. Educators hear a lot about making students productive members of society after they leave their schools. Be the educator who gives students the opportunity to be productive members of society *while* they are with you—from kindergarten on! The experience your students gain will be invaluable.

Showcasing beyond the refrigerator. Some say that when students create work to share on their refrigerator door, they make it "good enough," but when they are creating to share beyond the fridge, they will make it "good." Give students the opportunity to create and share their work beyond just their immediate family. Show them the power of sharing their *voice* with the world.

- *Create a podcast, blog, or vlog.* Students have a lot to say. They are super knowledgeable about a wide variety of topics: making slime, cooking the perfect steak, who the most sought-after Pokémon characters are, competitive eating—the list goes on and on! Pick any topic. Chances are someone in your classroom or school is an expert. Why not channel this energy and passion?! Let students create their own podcasts, blogs, or vlogs about those topics. Do you have any students who love to blog about video games? Guess what? They are writing and taking time to make sure people will view their blogs. To do this, they will make sure their blog is *good.* They will work at their writing craft and will probably learn a lot about web design, data analytics, and the power of sharing. The same goes for students who want to create food podcasts, talking about their latest cooking experiences, or the quiet students in the corner who go home every day and record vlogs about their favorite musicians. Having an authentic audience is incredibly meaningful for students.
- *The power of the portfolio.* How amazing would it be if students left your education system with a portfolio of their work? They would be able to demonstrate the growth they made during their time in your schools and would have a number of projects and activities demonstrating their passions. They would be able to share their finest writing, videos, photographs, drawings, books, and collaborative

works—or anything else that shows off their talent—with anyone who asks to see it. Students would be able to share the drawings of their pets they made in third grade, as well as the portraits of their grandparents that they completed in twelfth grade. In addition to sharing their work, reflecting on their own learning would also be powerful. The reality is, all the digital tools teachers now use with students make creating a portfolio rather easy to do. Let students authentically *create* and have them document their learning through a portfolio to serve as a reminder of their own learning process.

Service learning. One of the experiences I will always remember from high school is my visit to a local nursing home. We were required to complete a number of hours each year toward our service-learning goals. At the time, I remember going to the nursing home simply because my friends were going. But after spending a couple of hours visiting, talking, and walking around the grounds with the residents, I realized the experience was very much worth the time I was putting into it. I was leaving with an understanding of the need people have for human connections and companionship. I learned more about people than reading chapter eight in my book would have taught me. Sometimes, real life is better than the book.

- *Find those in need.* Our elementary school has a service club for any student in grades three through five who is interested in volunteer work. Parents and teachers help the members find worthwhile groups and activities in which to participate. Some of the tasks are simple: helping fold napkins and making place settings for a nearby soup kitchen or writing thank-you letters to the first responders in our area. Later in the year, the students will organize a soup drive for the local food pantry.

As I've already stated, plenty of individuals and organizations need help. Simply connect your students with the right groups so they can provide a helping hand and learn about something much larger than themselves in the process.

- *Support your community.* When thinking about service learning opportunities, remember some of those in need may be a part of your own community. Help students recognize their blessings and support those in need around them. You could involve students at an organized coat drive for fellow students in need or walk your high school students to the local elementary school to help with tutoring. To raise funds to donate to a local charity, students may want to organize a "One-Dollar Pajama Day"—even high school students will pay for the opportunity for extreme comfort—or a "Five-Dollar Debonair Day," which is the opposite of a dress-down day, where everyone dresses to the nines and wears their finest to show support. The possibilities are endless, both for the help students can provide *and* the learning taking place when they participate in these real-life experiences.

All in all, students will be more engaged when they are completing authentic work. They will be capable of solving previously unsolvable problems and making contributions beyond your classroom. Take time to find those real-life experiences to challenge students to extend their learning to places they've never gone before. Give them opportunities to share their expertise and brilliance with the world. Show them there is an audience who wants to hear what they have to say. As the "pirate" Dave Burgess says, "Provide an uncommon experience for your students, and they will reward you with uncommon effort and attitude."

SECRET SAUCE SUMMARY

- Students are more likely to engage in authentic learning activities when they have personal meaning and a connection to them.

- Let students connect, share, and collaborate with others around the world by using experiences like mystery calls, pen pals, or pairing up with another classroom.

- Give students the chance to solve real-world problems. Connect them with a community organization in need of help or let them tackle a problem your school community is struggling with.

- Showcase student work beyond the refrigerator. Technology now makes it easy for students to connect with a global audience, so allow students to create and share their content with the world.

- Let students engage in service learning. Providing a service to a local community organization or organizing a humanitarian drive to help people on the other side of the globe can give students a powerful and meaningful learning experience.

Planning and Reflecting

What kind of authentic learning opportunities are you currently providing for students?

_____

_____

_____

Are there other students your students can connect with? Do you know a teacher who lives in a different state or country? Is there a class across town who would want to participate in paired classroom activities?

_____

_____

_____

Do students have occasions to tackle authentic problems? What is an example of a real-world situation your students could address?

_____

_____

_____

How do your students share their work beyond your classroom? What other tools can you explore to help your students connect with a global audience?

_____

_____

_____

Could community organizations use your students' help? What groups could you partner with?

_____

_____

_____

Add Your Own SECRET SAUCE Ingredients

List three steps you will take to add authentic learning opportunities for your students.

1. _____

   _____

   _____

2. _____

   _____

   _____

3. _____

   _____

   _____

A Recipe for Success

Sick Days

I really wanted to title this section "How to Beat the Common Cold" or "Write *Awesome* Sub Plans That Work for Everyone!"

Think about the last commercial you saw for a cold medicine, the one where you see a miserably sick person who looks like death warmed over and can barely move from the bed. The voice-over begins to describe the symptoms: headache, runny nose, throat irritation, coughing, congestion, sneezing, fatigue, fever, body aches, sinus pressure, and of course, watery eyes. After the list of awful symptoms, the voice-over suggests the branded medicine, and the person on the screen somehow musters enough energy to take said medicine. Instantly, the person bounces back and is ready to tackle the day—by the end of the commercial!

Thirty seconds and the branded over-the-counter medicine have some kind of instant healing powers directly from a mystical shaman. I wish!

I'm not sure if you've ever experienced sickness in this way, but when I was a teacher, I had a completely different experience. It started with a slight cough, until a week later when it turned into a full-blown, can-barely-lift–my-head-off-the-pillow cold. All the while, I'd begrudgingly show up in my classroom every day because the alternative was every bit as awful. In fact, it was worse! I would rather drag myself in to work looking and feeling like a grotesque zombie than to do what all educators everywhere dread:

WRITE SUB PLANS!

[Dun-Dun-Duuuuun!]

NOOOOOOOOOOOOOOOOOOOOOOOOOOOOOOOOO!

Even though you are sick, when you write sub plans, you have to muster the energy to give a minute-by-minute account of what students should be doing throughout the entire day. You have to communicate who the troubled students are and which students can help in a pinch. You have to overplan just to keep the students from tying the substitute to a chair, but everything you plan is busywork. After all, you don't trust the substitute to teach anything new. You provide the name of a helpful teacher the substitute can go to, even though the substitutes tend to strike out on their own to decide what is best for the students they met just twenty minutes ago. As you struggle to write the plans, you wonder if this will be the day you *finally* end up with the *awesome* sub—the one who "gets" children, the one who doesn't have to employ temporary bribes and incentives to maintain control, the one who leaves your class at the end of the day without any problems. Yet, even with your pounding head, you realize the chance for this is unlikely, and you decide rather than put the effort into these plans and risk coming back to a bad report and three days of work to undo the one day you missed, it's just easier to drag yourself out of bed and struggle in to work.

Being ill doesn't have to be this way. You should be able to miss a day because you are sick, have a personal commitment required during school hours, or were "voluntold" to attend a district training. You shouldn't have to feel guilty or bad about missing time with your students.

This change actually starts by embracing the fact you *will* miss time in the classroom. Once you grasp this, the next goal is to get students to embrace opportunities when you are not with them.

After the first week or two of the school year, I introduced this idea to students with two simple questions:

- What would happen if I didn't show up one day?

- How would you learn on your own?

My goal as a teacher was to have my students so engaged in the learning process that if, for some reason, I didn't show up, they could continue learning on their own. No matter the skill set of the substitute involved, if you can get students to embrace this philosophy, you have done your part as an educator. Students who continue their learning process in the absence of their teacher is a sign of an *exceptional* teacher. It means you have established an environment where the learning process is beautiful and exciting, breathtaking and necessary, and vital to the learner's existence. Nothing can stop learning from taking place, even the absence of the teacher. It shouldn't matter if the teacher doesn't show up one day. The learning goes on no matter what.

At the beginning of the year, this goal has more to do with the students learning routines and procedures so they can internalize them. If you are not there, will they know how to complete daily tasks? After modeling and a great deal of practice, students eventually can complete classroom routines and procedures without any prompting.

By the end of the year, the goal shifts to ensuring students can drive their own learning. If you don't show up, how will students continue their learning? What will they do to continue their growth as a learner? This is a lot more difficult to accomplish than students internalizing routines because it asks students to reach a state of intrinsic motivation. Students are asked to learn for the sake of learning—the ultimate goal of every classroom.

So how do you create this type of environment where students want to learn despite your absence?

Begin by asking, "What will you do if I don't show up?" Explain your goal. Explain what the learning process should look like, both when you are in the classroom and when you are not there. (Hint: It should look the same!) In the student-centered classroom, students hold the power over the learning process, and the teacher helps facilitate. Be sure students know and understand this.

Model, model, model. Practice, practice, practice. Be sure to dedicate plenty of time for students to learn and practice routines during the first four to six weeks of school. Hold students to high expectations and focus on modeling the types of behaviors you would like to see from them. Who can students go to if they need help when you are not there? How do students communicate they need help? What resources have you put in place for when students require assistance? What routines are in place for students to own their learning process? What does a student do if he or she needs a pencil? How do groups rotate during centers or stations? Thinking about *every* situation that could potentially arise is impossible, but the goal of practicing these routines ad nauseam is to create self-motivated, self-sufficient learners.

Build a culture supporting student ownership and empowerment. Rome was not built in a day, and neither is your classroom culture. You—and your students—will have to work at it. You will need to spend time on those routines and procedures. You will constantly need to provide opportunities for students to lead and take responsibility for what happens in the classroom. If something goes wrong for a student, don't instantly solve the problem for them. Get used to asking, "How will you fix it?" Empower students to find solutions and make decisions by providing support for them to carry out those decisions. When a classroom is truly student-centered, it should be humming with productivity, meaningful learning, creation, and consumption, whether you are there or not. Students need to be in charge every day, not just days when you are absent.

Write your sub plans for students. If your class is truly learner-centric, students should be readily taking on an equal share of work. Your sub plans should reflect this. Writing your plans for students allows them to have a clear expectation as to why they should be taking ownership of their learning. It puts the responsibility on them and puts them in the driver's seat. If your classroom runs this way when you are there, students will make an easy transition when you are gone. Simply provide your students with a list of meaningful activities they should be working on and a list of resources available to help them further their learning. Make sure students, just like the substitute teacher, have copies of the plans.

IMPORTANT REMINDER: Creating this type of environment will only work if you have already ceded control of your classroom to your students. If you normally are largely responsible for solving all of the problems in the classroom, students will not suddenly be able to own their learning when you are not there. Remember all of the hard work taking place when you are *not* there is built upon all of the hard work taking place when you *are* there.

Chapter 9

UTILITY IN CLASSROOM DESIGN

Everything is designed. Few things are designed well.

—BRIAN REED

What You Need to Know: Consider utility in your classroom design. Make sure your learning space matches your learning goals.

At one time, I was extremely focused on what my classroom looked like. I spent almost a week in August preparing it for the first day of school. Motivational posters, math rules, and science facts. Extension activities. Almost all of the wall space was covered, although I did leave a small portion of one wall to hang student work later in the year. I didn't put any real thought into it, though. I just knew a successful classroom was well decorated.

As I watched my colleagues, I saw some who worked even harder at decorating than I did. They might spend two weeks setting up their classrooms before students returned. Some might even show up days before the official teacher-start date and weeks before the official student-start date in order to get their classrooms ready. After several years of teaching, I began to believe

Parkinson's law was at work: the activity would always expand to fill the amount of time allotted for it. If you allot two weeks to set up your classroom, it will take you two weeks to set up your classroom. If you only allot two days, it will only take two days. You always find a way to use the time you allot.

I never gave classroom design much thought in those early years. Sure, I made some conscious decisions about the classroom, but it wasn't important to me. It took me a while, in fact, to figure out why it is important for students.

The first time I really thought about *intentional* classroom design was when I became an administrator. I was hired as an elementary supervisor responsible for overseeing all curriculum and instruction in four kindergarten-through-fifth-grade buildings. On the first day of school for students, I was visiting classrooms with another administrator. About halfway through our visit, we entered one classroom and were completely shocked. Upon opening the door, we realized the classroom walls were completely bare.

Not a single poster. Not a single decoration. Nothing.

Empty, bare, white walls.

All the classroom decorations were lying in a pile on a table.

As my colleague and I left the room, we chalked it up to an unprepared teacher. Nothing was done because the teacher had made the decision *not* to arrive before school began and prepare like the rest of her colleagues. Maybe she was lazy. Maybe she was completely overwhelmed. Regardless, she had definitely made an intentional decision. While my colleague felt it was simply unacceptable, I wasn't sure what to think. Would someone really choose *not* to decorate her room?

We decided to circle back to this classroom before we left the building. We wanted to ask the teacher *when* the room would be decorated.

Her response?

"I let the *students* decide what gets hung on the wall."

It now became crystal clear to me. This explained the pile of posters on the table and the empty, sterile walls. She had made an intentional decision—an intentional decision about classroom design. As I drove home, I thought long and hard about the teacher's answer. Was it more important that the students had a say in the classroom or that the classroom looked warm and inviting as students walked in? While I couldn't quite figure out how I felt about it, I realized maybe there was more to classroom design than I had ever really considered.

SECRET SAUCE Ingredient

Neat orderly rows of desks may work well for you, but they do not work well for students. If you need to have desks in your classroom, consider grouping them in a cluster so students can be more collaborative. Remember, however, that some students may still need some privacy. Plan to have a single desk for any student who may need it at any given time.

Tables versus Chairs

As I reflected, I realized I had also made intentional decisions about classroom design. When I was in the classroom, I taught two groups of fifth-graders. I did a math lesson and science lesson in the morning, and I repeated them in the afternoon. One of the problems I faced early on was a lack of space for any type of real science experimentation. In my first year, my mentor was a special education teacher who taught a group of thirteen fourth- and fifth-graders. Her advice was invaluable to me. She brought her students into my morning class for science each day. This was great for me. If I was not familiar with a concept or was uncomfortable explaining something, she jumped in and we would co-teach. It was a great experience to have in my first year—except for one thing.

When her thirteen students joined my twenty-seven students, we had forty students! (I double-checked the math twice, just to be sure.) In addition, she came along with three paraprofessionals, meaning a total of five adults were also in the room. Were there really forty-five people in the room?

Again, I double-checked the math: 27 + 13 + 5 = ?

Seven plus three, carry the one, plus five more…

You get the idea. Suffice it to say, 27 + 13 + 5 equaled a whole lot of teachers and students in my room for science each day!

We were supposed to be doing hands-on science lessons, but we didn't have enough chairs or desks for the students. Many of the kids who traveled into the classroom each day had to cram at a table. They also had to make the trek each day with their books *and* a chair. As you can imagine, the conditions were less than ideal. But these are the moments when you grow and learn as an educator, if you take the time to reflect. Toward the end of this first year, I began to think about my second year. I even kept a list in a notebook of "Things to Do in Year Two."

One thing I noticed was all of our most successful science lessons had us using tables. When we modeled something, we gathered the students around the two tables in the room. When students worked at the tables, they had more space and were able to collaborate more on experiments. While I didn't realize it at the time, I was consciously thinking about classroom design.

I started by asking my principal if my desks could be replaced with tables for my second year, but she didn't have the money to do it. So I kept at it. I continued to explain the benefits of having tables versus desks in the classroom. Kids would be able to collaborate and share more often. Classroom management would be easier. Kids would actually need to be more organized. (I wasn't sure if any of these things would actually happen, but I tried to convince her they would!) As I continued to get *no* after no, I began to push my idea and reasoning on our assistant principal, who left our building to become a principal shortly after. I don't think it was because of my constant table requests, though!

After a few years of begging and pleading, met by continued *no*'s, I knew I was going to have to either give up my dream of tables or go rogue. If you know me, you can probably guess what I did. Each classroom in my building had desks and two tables. We had more than thirty classrooms, so I began to work out separate side deals with several teachers. *If I give you a few desks, would you be willing to give up a table?* A few were willing to trade the table straight up for four desks. Some felt bad for me and offered their tables without requiring an exchange. Some tried to negotiate shrewdly as if they were the general manager of a sports team at the trade deadline. When all was said and done, I was ready to add five tables to my room but only lose twelve desks.

If you ever want to maneuver such a change, this is the important part to remember: only after I procured the move of the tables to my room did I go to the principal and change my tact. I no longer asked for new tables. I simply asked if I could have tables if some of my colleagues were willing to trade them with me. After a couple of years, I think she was tired of hearing from me, and she agreed, with the condition that all of the desks in my room found a home. This is where it pays to become good friends with your building custodians. I talked to our floor custodian about my desk and table situation, and he agreed to help me move the desks out of my room and the tables in. But I had one more obstacle to overcome: eighteen additional desks no one wanted. Luckily, he helped me find a secret storage room in the bowels of the building and assured me no one would ever know if the desks ended up in there. So I stacked those desks in the corner of the hidden room, and, for all I know, they may still be there today!

(Shout out to Everett here! He is one of the best custodians I have ever worked with.)

Finally, I had tables in my room. My goal of collaboration and interactive lessons would be realized! More importantly, though, I learned classroom design has to be about utility.

When Resources Are Limited

Maybe you want to make drastic changes in your learning space, but your resources are limited. You might not have any tables available but more desks than you can count. You might have a limited budget. You might not have a lot of space. Don't fear. Lots of options for improving your learning space still exist, even with limited resources.

Take a look at the following problems and solutions:

I have no tables in my classroom and too many desks. Use the desks to *make* tables. Group desks so students can work collaboratively. Four or six desks can easily be pushed together to create a "table." What's great about this option is you can also vary your "table" designs from time to time. This week work in groups of four; next week, work with "mini-tables" composed of two student desks. Having a group discussion? Make a long table with a series of student desks facing one another.

I don't have much money to dedicate to improving my learning space. Even if you are seriously lacking cash, you can still improve your space. Reach out to local businesses and ask for donations. They are likely to donate to schools. A donated picnic table, for example, can serve as an excellent outside learning space when placed in the right spot. Or go to your local office supply store and ask them to donate clipboards. Students suddenly have a workspace they can take anywhere! You can also ask parents to send in older furniture to possibly work into your classroom. Explain to parents what you are trying to accomplish and ask for donations. Think about small benches, beach chairs, stools, yoga balls, etcetera.

I have a small classroom and lack any real space. The key is to find some more space or maximize the space you do have. Hallways outside of classrooms can be utilized at a cost of zero dollars. Hang up a whiteboard right outside your classroom door and turn it into an extension of your learning space. Also consider addition by subtraction. If you have a small classroom to begin with, analyze your space and decide if you need everything you have. Often those extra bins of "teacher stuff" you've accumulated or inherited might not be necessary. The rule here is simple: if you or students are not using it, get rid of it.

Remember, if you truly want to improve your learning space, you may need to beg, borrow, and steal. No, okay, don't steal. But you absolutely can *beg* and *borrow*! Find teachers who are leaving their classroom for a different position or getting ready for retirement and no longer need the furniture they have amassed over the years. Ask for donations or write a grant proposal. Ask for volunteers who might be able to build new furniture or fix old furniture. Get rid of the stuff you don't need. Hit garage sales on the weekends. Do whatever needed to make the learning space work for you and your students.

Designing Your Classroom

As a designer, you need to ask yourself one question: *what are you trying to accomplish in your learning space?*

Conscious decisions must go into the learning spaces you are creating for students or, better yet, students are creating for themselves. Take a moment and think about your learning space. What does it say about your expectations of the learning taking place? If you are a new teacher, think about your goals for students. What do you want them to accomplish and how can the learning environment help them reach those goals? If you are an experienced teacher, take an inventory of your classroom. Is it set up in a way to help students be more productive, or are there barriers to learning inherent in the design of the classroom?

SECRET SAUCE Ingredient

Simple fixes can go a long way in your classroom. Consider asking your custodian to raise or lower the legs on a table to make students feel more comfortable. Raising the legs on a table makes it a great standing table for students. Lowering the legs makes it a great workspace for students who are more comfortable on the floor. You don't have to put forth a lot of time or effort in order to improve your learning space.

Asking questions about your classroom can help you think deeply about the learning space. Start with the following questions:

Is there enough open space and white space? Students often need a great deal of space. They have a lot of stuff. Open space is easier to transition based on the learning activity students are working on. Additionally, too many colors, posters, charts, and other cutesy materials can be overstimulating for students. Leave enough white space for students to feel comfortable adding to the learning environment.

Are you utilizing all of the space available to you? Many learning spaces are incredibly small. In order to use your space effectively, you may have to think about other usable spaces. Classroom design expert Bob Dillon calculates that a third of all square footage in schools is hallway space. How can your students utilize the hallway? Put tables and stools right outside your classroom door. A whiteboard in the hallway outside your classroom serves as a fantastic learning space, as well. (See? It doesn't have to be expensive! A four-by-eight-feet sheet of shower board from your local hardware supply chain can be purchased for less than $20! If you tell them you are of the "noblest profession," and you want the shower board for your students, they may even give it to you for free. It has worked for me!)

Do students have choices allowing them to be comfortable? And now, a story about one of my former students. Jason was in one of my first fifth-grade classes. After three weeks of school, I realized he couldn't sit still. He was constantly standing at his desk to work and blocking the view of students behind him. Multiple times a day, I was arguing with him to sit down so the other students in the class could see. It took me nearly five months to realize I should just put his desk at the back of the classroom so he could stand whenever he wanted or needed to.

You would be surprised how much more will be accomplished by students who feel comfortable in their learning space. Consider different seating options. Raise the legs on your tables so students can stand at them if they need to. Let students lie on the floor or huddle in a corner if they want to. Giving them options to feel comfortable can help students take ownership of the learning space.

Promote Movement in the Classroom

Students spend multiple hours in your classroom every day. Movement should be a natural part of the day for students *and* teachers. In *Teaching with the Brain in Mind*, Eric Jensen points to research findings that indicate that student learning improves because of the link between mind and body and says, "Movement activities should become as important as so-called 'book work.'"

Do your students spend the majority of their time in your classroom sitting in their seats?

Try these ideas to incorporate more movement into your students' days:

Take a brain break. Teachers and students in our school district have fallen in love with GoNoodle (gonoodle.com). The website provides musical videos and physical activities to get students up and out of their seats. Dancing and singing along, students get a brain break and will be better able to focus and improve their academic performance. This interactive website uses group incentives to motivate students to take part in daily activity.

Take a walk. Are students stuck for ideas in your classroom? Encourage them to take a walk. Steve Jobs, among others, was famous for his long walks, using the sojourns to problem-solve, think, and sometimes hold meetings. Giving students a chance to get out of their seat and take a quick walk through the halls can help students get the creative juices flowing. Sometimes a change of location can help students see a problem in a different way or think differently about an assignment.

Switch up your grouping. One of the easiest ways to incorporate more movement is to give students multiple collaborative grouping opportunities throughout the day. Use the Random Name Picker (flippity.net) to create groups of two, three, or more. Have students work with one partner and then switch to another, as if speed dating. Give students multiple chances to get out of their seats to work with a variety of partners during class.

Encourage students to be comfortable. Where do students sit in your class? Set up a multitude of seating options within your classroom, allowing students to be comfortable. Stability balls are a great active option for students. Find an exercise bike at a yard sale or ask the PTA to donate one. Create different seating options and settings within your room to encourage movement and activity with students.

Consider yoga. Many teachers are incorporating mindfulness into their lessons now. Consider using elements of yoga to help students center themselves before daily lessons. Breathing exercises and yoga poses can help students relax, and even help reduce stress prior to a test. Use relaxation techniques to help yourself as the teacher and model for students. Create a more peaceful, calmer setting to help students improve performance.

Does your learning space coincide with your learning goals? Design your classroom with your overarching learning goals in mind. Want students to be more collaborative? Then you should probably have tables in your room where students can collaborate. Want students to really experience a love of reading? Make sure you have plenty of comfortable, cozy reading nooks so students can enjoy curling up with a good book. In middle and high schools, 360-degree math classes are now popping up, where students are surrounded on all sides by whiteboards. Students solve problems while standing at the whiteboards for the entire class period. In this classroom, lessons are focused entirely on math learning, and the design of the classroom matches that objective.

Is the lighting or color palette within your space impacting student mood? Early in my career, I had never considered whether the lighting in the room or the color of the walls had any impact on student learning outcomes. After listening to some experts talk about the impact these design elements can have, though, I completely changed my mind. Learning spaces including a lot of natural light can help students. Students may feel more or less comfortable depending on the brightness or darkness of the room. Bob Dillon has also shared that educators want to avoid the classroom looking like a bag of Skittles. Too many colors and patterns can cause overstimulation for students.

Would students say it is YOUR classroom or THEIR classroom? When asked, students can be brutally honest. If you asked them who the classroom belonged to, how would they answer? Students should feel comfortable in the classroom. They should feel as if their opinions are valued, and they have a *voice* in what goes on and how the room is set up. Don't let your learning space be dominated by teacher materials or your stuff. Make sure it is open to students and their needs.

Are materials easily accessible to students so they can be self-reliant? The goal of every classroom should be for students to demonstrate varying degrees of independence in order to take ownership of their learning. This starts by providing students with the opportunity to manage materials and routines in the classroom. Can students easily find and access the materials they need? Do they have to ask the teacher for help to use those materials or can they freely work on their own? Helping students easily access materials and resources also allows the teacher to conduct more meaningful work, like conferencing with a student one-on-one or working with a small group.

Does your workspace provide flexibility? Some days students may be working independently; other days, they may work in collaborative groups. This may even happen in the space of one class period. The room needs to be flexible enough to allow students to switch easily between activities and learning modes. Easily movable furniture works great for these types of situations.

Why do you need a teacher's desk? Try to avoid having your thumbprint over everything within your learning space. Teachers who take up a lot of space are leaving less area for students. Start with your teacher's desk. Do you really need it? Chances are, it is a large monstrosity taking up a great deal of real estate, and you may hardly sit there throughout the day. Most teachers will be up and active, circulating among students during an activity. If you absolutely must have a space for your stuff, consider placing your materials in a closet. At the very least, tuck your desk into a corner facing a wall in order to maximize the learning space. Remember the principle of "our" classroom versus "my" classroom. The teacher's desk screams, "This is *my* classroom!"

Few things can be as daunting as walking into your empty classroom for the first time and trying to figure out what it should look like. Remember, you want the learning space to match your learning goals for students. What do you want students to accomplish? How can the learning space be designed to help you accomplish those goals? As you approach classroom design, work with what you have. Make decisions based on what works for you, but more importantly, on what works for your students. Don't focus on making the learning space look pretty or appealing. Make the learning space functional!

The Classroom Design Checklist

Create spaces to promote collaboration.
- ❏ Tables
- ❏ Desks grouped together
- ❏ Chairs facing one another
- ❏ Whiteboard spaces for design

Give students a variety of seating options.
- ❏ High tables for standing
- ❏ Low tables for sitting on the floor
- ❏ Chairs
- ❏ Stools
- ❏ Benches
- ❏ Anything students feel comfortable sitting on

Make materials easily accessible.
- ❏ Design with the workflow in mind.
- ❏ Let students decide what their workflow will be before a final spot is chosen for materials.
- ❏ Put materials and resources at student height.

Consider the lighting in your room.
- ❏ Making it too bright or keeping it too dark will impact students negatively.
- ❏ Let as much natural light into the classroom as possible.
- ❏ Use several small lamps around the classroom to create a warm atmosphere.

Consider the color scheme in your room.
- ❏ Use one or two primary colors with basic accents.
- ❏ Don't overdo it with color.
- ❏ When in doubt, keep it simple.

Leave plenty of whitespace for students.
- ❏ Space for student work
- ❏ Space for anchor charts
- ❏ Writable space for students
- ❏ Walls without clutter

Don't dominate the real estate as the teacher.
- ❏ Minimize the amount of learning space you use.
- ❏ Get rid of your teacher desk or, at the very least, hide it in a corner.
- ❏ Utilize a corner of a table or a closet to keep your most important things.
- ❏ Utilize a laptop device and get rid of the desktop in your classroom.

Take advantage of all available space.
- ❏ Nooks and crannies
- ❏ Hallways
- ❏ Stages, cafeteria, or auditorium spaces
- ❏ Under your desk (now tucked into the corner)

Provide flexibility as you set up the classroom.
- ❏ Use easily movable furniture or pieces on wheels.
- ❏ Take advantage of areas designed to be used for multiple activities, such as a carpeted meeting area for elementary students or a table where older students can gather for directions.

SECRET SAUCE SUMMARY

- Think critically about intentional classroom design.

- Even with limited resources, consider the small changes that can be made to improve your learning space.

- Think deeply about your learning space by asking specific design questions. Always remember that the classroom design should be based on your classroom goals.

- Design your classroom to allow for movement within the learning space. Give students the opportunity to get up and out of their seats to inspire learning.

- Use only what is necessary in your classroom. If you don't use it, get rid of it!

Planning and Reflecting

Does your learning space match your learning goals for students? How can you improve the space to better match your goals?

_____

_____

_____

_____

How will you involve students in the classroom design?

_____

_____

_____

_____

What materials are you working with? What space is available? How can you use these more effectively?

_____

_____

_____

_____

Consider _less is more._ What can you remove from your learning space to improve overall functionality?

_____

_____

_____

_____

Are students comfortable working in the space you have created? What did you do to help them feel comfortable? What can you do to help them feel _more_ comfortable?

_____

_____

_____

_____

Add Your Own SECRET SAUCE Ingredients

List three actions you will take to improve your learning space.

1. _____

_____

_____

2. _____

_____

_____

3. _____

_____

_____

Chapter 10

CONNECTIONS

Isolation is now a choice educators make.

—GEORGE COUROS

What You Need to Know: Connecting with other educators both inside and outside your school setting can help you challenge your notions of education, ask questions, and continue to grow as a professional.

Connections Are Critical

When I first started teaching, I was lucky to get connected with my partner-in-crime, Trevor Bryan. Although I didn't realize it at the time, Trevor would become the person I turned to throughout my first several years in education to challenge my assumptions and get me to think deeply about my *why*. Trevor was the art teacher who worked with my fifth-grade students. We dreamed up big ideas and then did our best to implement them, often having to scale back because the ideas were simply *too* big. Once we decided the generic, cheesy pictures taken on picture day—think laser backgrounds!—didn't quite capture who our fifth-grade students truly were. Trevor and I decided we could do a better job with a digital camera, a simple black cloth backdrop, and some natural light. We set up a makeshift studio in my classroom in the back corner near a window and taught the students some basics about photography. The students worked for nearly two months to capture the "essence" of their classmates. The portraits turned out to be beautiful statements about who our students were, and we even had students write about who they were as a person. Trevor purchased frames through a grant, opened up a student art gallery on the second floor of our school building, and our first annual Family Gallery Night was born.

Parents and other family members came to see the photos, dine on some cheese and crackers and juice—no wine for this gallery opening!—and enjoy the meaningful portraits the students had created. After we finished displaying the portraits in the gallery, each student got to take their portrait (taken by a classmate) with them, and several parents framed the pictures to hang at home as the quality of the portraits was akin to what might be done at a professional studio.

I never would have come up with such a project on my own. The power of connecting with someone else who challenged my thinking allowed me to become part of such an amazing project. And so it went until I decided to move along in my career to become an administrator, and my opportunities to connect and converse with Trevor slowly diminished. Other educators filled in for a while, lending a hand to challenge me and question why I was doing something. I still talked to Trevor on a regular basis, but it was never quite the same (until later when technology changed everything!).

When I was fully entrenched in my first administrative role, I felt an apathy and loneliness I hadn't felt as an educator before. I felt somewhat isolated; I wasn't connecting with the right people. I needed to be pushed, and I had no one to push me. I experienced an extreme sense of malaise. I had never experienced this in my career before, and I wasn't sure what to do about it. Simply put, I was stuck in a rut, and I needed something to change. Still, I wasn't expecting what came next. I discovered that there were other educators on Twitter willing to connect and share. As I look back, I realize it was such a gradual change I didn't recognize the impact it was having on me at the time; however, connecting with other educators via social media completely shifted my trajectory as an educator.

Educators used to talk with their grade-level counterparts or subject-area team during a common planning period for forty minutes. Then they returned to their classrooms and closed their doors. The most progressive of educators may have read a monthly journal, from where they pulled ideas and shared them with colleagues. When I discovered Twitter, I didn't realize another world of education existed out there. I didn't realize how many other "connected" educators were on social media, willing to share the ideas and resources making them successful.

As I stated, I had felt isolated in my position. I had become a first-time administrator, traveling between several buildings each week without ever planting my feet solidly among one community of learners. In all of my previous positions, I had a person to challenge my thinking. So I reached out to other educators on Twitter, ultimately, leading me to becoming a better educator.

The ability to connect exists for everyone. Whether you are the sole music or physical education teacher in your building, part of a team of two at your grade level, or the only German teacher in your district, you can find others who share your passions, commiserate with your struggles, and seek the same solutions you are searching for. The world has become increasingly small, and it is now easier than ever to connect with the experts—other educators who will help you grow.

I recently had the opportunity to speak with a group of under-grad Education majors. Many of them were juniors and seniors in college, preparing for their student-teaching experiences or preparing to interview for their first teaching jobs. I shared many of the topics and ideas from this book to inspire the young educators to be the best they could be. At the end of my speech, I wanted to promote a #CoffeeEDU session coming up at their university just a couple of weeks later. I spoke of the potential to connect with other smart, established educators: principals, superintendents, curriculum supervisors, and other teachers they could learn from. Prior to finishing my pitch, I added this caveat: "As college students, a start time of 7:00 a.m. on Sunday might be a bit too early for many of you because of other priorities you may have."

Ironically, while speaking about the power of connecting, I completely underestimated the future educators. I couldn't have been more wrong! The students showed up in full force to share, collaborate, and connect at the #CoffeeEDU session. They asked brilliant questions, contributed excellent ideas, and grew as professionals. The other educators at the session also learned a great deal about those about to enter the profession, and I learned a valuable lesson about not underestimating people. To those about to rock a classroom, we salute you!

Remember, human beings are social. They want to connect, share, talk, discuss, network and interface, and join in what others are doing. As educators, your need to do this is doubly as strong because many of you work with children all day. Some of you don't have the chance to speak with another adult for several hours at a time, and the need to be a part of what other educators are building is compelling.

Connecting with Others

How can you connect with others?

Start with those who will help you grow. One of the biggest mistakes in my career was assuming my administrators were the only ones who could help me grow as an educator. I always thought they would be the ones to provide professional learning opportunities or impart some sort of wisdom to me, and then I'd be a better educator. While I did work with some great administrators over the years who taught me a lot, I've realized this doesn't necessarily have to be the case. As an educator, you need to find the *exact* people who will help you grow—and they are all around. Your "exact" person might be a fellow teacher from down the hall, an instructional coach, or a curriculum supervisor who visits the building occasionally. It might not be the person you assume will help you learn the most. It could also be someone outside of your school environment, but if they are not in your building, you may have to seek them out.

If you learn best from the math supervisor who only makes it to your building twice a month, for example, you may have to e-mail him or her with specific questions or travel to the workshops he or she hosts elsewhere. Remember, *your* growth is *your* responsibility. You must find those who are going to help you grow. Learn from them. Share with them. Collaborate with them. Let them challenge you. Be accountable to them. Let them ask if you can do better. Spend the majority of your time with them.

But be aware—and this is crucial—you will also come in contact with people who will stunt your growth. Avoid those who don't help you grow. Don't let them drain your energy. Associate only with those who are going to make you better.

Engage with and emulate the best teacher you know. As you are seeking those who will help you grow, you will come across many exceptional educators—perhaps someone on your grade-level team or someone in your department, or maybe someone who teaches a completely different subject. (If you recall, as a math and science teacher, I actually learned the most from an art teacher!)

Regardless, when you figure out who the best educators are, engage with and emulate them.

- *Ask questions.* This profession is about standing on the shoulders of giants and learning from those who came before. No question is a dumb question when you are trying to learn from someone else.
  - How did you come up with your lesson?
  - Why are your students so well-behaved in the hallways and cafeteria?
  - I notice you assess in various ways instead of giving a chapter quiz or unit test each week. How do you manage this?
- *Spend time in other classrooms.* One of the limitations to learning from the best teachers you know is that you won't be able to find time to learn from them. Unfortunately, it is usually difficult to visit other classrooms to learn. *Make the time to do it.* If you have a prep period, find out who is teaching during this time and go observe them. Ask permission first and tell the person why you are interested in visiting. If it is not a possibility, ask if an administrator would be willing to cover your class or provide coverage for a period while you visit another classroom. Ask if there is an extra substitute period during the day, giving you the opportunity to get out of your classroom and see other educators in action. It can be a phenomenal learning experience.
- *Imitation is the sincerest form of flattery.* Once you see other successful instructional practices, emulate them.

Take something working for someone else and try it out in your classroom. Maybe you need to tweak it slightly because you are working with different students or because it doesn't quite fit within your teaching style, but when you see successful practices to possibly work into your classroom, don't be afraid to steal them.

As a young teacher, I was given the opportunity to team-teach in an inclusion classroom. While I wasn't sure who I would be partnered with, I was thrilled to have the chance to work daily with another teacher. The team approach allowed me to watch another teacher tackle lessons while I observed and learned. When I saw something my co-teacher did during a lesson, I would try it out on my own. It didn't always work, but it was a great way to help me learn how to teach. While it was a unique learning opportunity—the option to team-teach in such a setting doesn't present itself very often!—it provided the base for me to grow tremendously as an educator.

Extend your Professional Learning Network. Finding those to help you grow might mean looking outside your own district. Many experts are out there, excited to share and ready to collaborate and learn alongside you, but you may have to take the next step to connect with these educators. In going beyond your grade-level team, department, or Professional Learning Community (PLC), you may find other educators who challenge your notion of what instruction can look like. You may find some amazing ideas to implement in your own classroom. You may find your educational kindred spirit, even though he teaches roughly three thousand miles away from you. The power of the #PLN (Professional Learning Network) can take you to the next level as an educator.

- *Connect with other passionate educators through social media.* If you have not participated in Twitter as a teacher, you are missing out on one of the most powerful professional development tools available. At any time, 24-7, you can log on and borrow ideas from other teachers in the trenches who are doing phenomenal work with students in their classrooms. Follow other educators you find doing meaningful work. Interact with them, ask questions, and challenge yourself to become a better educator. Just like in real life, avoid those who suck your energy away!

- *Go beyond the character limits of Twitter.* Share your voice—literally—using the Voxer app. Voxer is a walkie-talkie app allowing you to share asynchronous voice messages with anyone around the world. And it is completely *free.* Many Voxer groups exist to talk on a daily basis about relevant and meaningful education topics. Connecting with educators outside your district on Voxer can provide an alternative perspective, different opinions, and a multitude of other ways to do things.

The Voxer group #4OCFpln grew out of an online book study of *The Four O'Clock Faculty.* After four weeks of discussing the book, the amazing educators in this group wanted to continue the daily discussions because they were learning so much. After more than a year, the group is still going strong and commits daily to engaging in important conversations about education. They ask difficult questions, think on a higher level, and commit to bringing their learning back to the classroom in order to do what's best for students. Finding a group of educators like this can really change your trajectory as a teacher. It's as simple as connecting!

The experts are out there. They are just waiting to connect! For most great teachers, geeking out about instructional strategies, content, or pedagogy is extremely fun. Don't hide in your room. Don't ever feel like you are isolated. Remember, isolation is a choice for educators. Plenty of people will help you grow. You just may need to seek them out. They may not be in your building or district, and they may be the last people you expected to help you, but if you make those connections, you have the opportunity to learn and grow as a professional.

SECRET SAUCE SUMMARY

- Connecting with other educators can help you grow as a teacher.

- Other educators are willing to share, collaborate, and help you grow. You just have to reach out to them. Every day, technology makes it increasingly easier to connect with others.

- Seek out those who will help you grow and avoid those who will sap your energy and keep you stagnant.

- Spend time in different classrooms observing how others teach. Ask questions, and try to emulate what you see other teachers doing.

- Extend your Professional Learning Network. Use social media to connect with other passionate educators and experts who are willing to share the great work they are doing.

Planning and Reflecting

Who are the best teachers you know? How can you find time to visit their classrooms or ask them questions?

_____

_____

_____

Are there other educators who you can learn from? Who are the people you may not see every day who can help you? Make a list and reach out to them.

_____

_____

_____

What is the best lesson you have observed recently? If you haven't observed a lesson recently, whose class can you visit to see a lesson?

_____

_____

_____

How can you expand your Professional Learning Network? How can you connect with educators outside your school or district?

_____

_____

_____

What lesson have you "stolen" from a colleague? What went well during your version of the lesson? What did you have to tweak in order to make it work for you?

_____

_____

_____

Add Your Own SECRET SAUCE Ingredients

List three actions you will take to make connections with other passionate educators.

1. _____

_____

_____

2. _____

_____

_____

3. _____

_____

_____

A Recipe for Success

Professional and Personal Growth

In *The Four O'Clock Faculty: A ROGUE Guide to Revolutionizing Professional Development*, I detailed my struggle to get what I needed in terms of professional learning as a new teacher. The biggest mistake I made was leaving the responsibility of my professional growth up to someone else. I was terribly disappointed when I didn't get what I needed. I assumed my building administrators and district administrators who were planning professional development were thinking about what I needed. Sometimes they were overwhelmed with providing professional development to the large groups of teachers they were working with—more than a dozen brand-new teachers in my building alone. While I realize now there is no way each educator will get exactly what he or she needs in a scenario like this, at the time I waited, never understanding I needed to take charge of my own growth.

I don't want you to make the same mistake. Many opportunities exist for you to get what you need. Many opportunities are out there for you to get what you *want*. You can grow professionally in such a way to get what you want *and* need while also meeting the overarching professional development goals of your school or district.

Here are some things you can try in order to take charge of your own professional growth.

Create your own professional development. Sometimes you will have an amazing professional learning experience at a session provided by your school district. Sometimes you will *not*. It may be necessary for you to go rogue and find your own professional development. Plenty of opportunities are out there.

- *Visit edcamp.org/edcamp-locations to find the latest Edcamp near you.* If you have never experienced Edcamp, it is a gathering of passionate educators who drive the professional learning by creating and choosing the sessions throughout the day. It is the ultimate in educator voice and choice. Want to learn more about student-centered instruction or social-emotional learning? Someone at Edcamp can probably help.

- *Join a #CoffeeEDU (coffeeedu.org/guidelines) group.* These informal events can be planned by anyone, but they usually involve a number of educators getting together on a Saturday or Sunday morning at a local coffeehouse or other casual establishment to discuss relevant education topics. For an hour, educators can share and learn in an informal, no-pressure setting with no set agenda. It's a great way to connect with other like-minded educators, and the discussions taking place at these events can often inspire you to improve learning outcomes for students in the classroom.

- *Offer to present or share at your next staff meeting.* I'll let you in on one of the biggest secrets in education: your administrator would *love* for you to take responsibility for planning the next staff meeting. Host an Appy Hour (fouroclockfaculty.com/2018/05/guest-post-appy-hour), model a lesson, or lead a #StaffBookTasting (fouroclockfaculty.com/2018/01/staffbooktasting). Spend the time productively. Give your colleagues something to get excited about, and take the pressure off of your building administrators to carry the responsibility of getting professional development right for each individual educator in your building.

Discover education blogs. Many educators these days are detailing both their successes and their struggles for the world to see. If you take a few minutes each week to read several blog posts, you may find a lesson idea to resonate with your students, you may stumble upon a solution to your motivation woes for a particular student, or you may be able to commiserate with another educator who is experiencing the same struggles you are. When an educator shares her story well, you can learn a lot about how to improve your own teaching. Some of my favorite education blogs include the following:

- *DITCH That Textbook* (ditchthattextbook.com) is a blog in which Matt Miller shares ideas for incorporating technology seamlessly into your lessons to improve learning or to make things easier. He always has many easy-to-follow ideas that can be implemented in the classroom.
- *Cult of Pedagogy* (cultofpedagogy.com) is where "Teacher nerds, unite!" Jennifer Gonzalez discusses specific lesson ideas, asks important questions about teaching practices, and provides strategies for finding balance as an educator. The blog posts are often coupled with podcasts where the ideas are discussed further.
- *Instant Relevance* (denissheeran.com) presents lesson ideas connected to what's happening in the world. Denis Sheeran, who is a math geek like me, finds a way to make learning relevant to current events and the things students are actually interested in—perhaps a unit of study to go along with the Olympics, some lesson ideas related to the Super Bowl, or a discussion on the true shape of snowflakes.

- *Edutopia* (edutopia.org) combines practical teaching strategies and ideas. It inspires using personal stories and innovative practices in order to improve education. The blog features a variety of educators sharing their voices in order to help all teachers become better for students.

Explore podcasts. I used to commute almost three hours round trip. It was a lot of time spent in a vehicle. I'll repeat, a *lot* of time. I had to find a way *not* to waste the time I spent driving. (See Chapter 6!) Enter podcasts. If you have not discovered the world of podcasts, the simple explanation is these are audio recordings you can listen to on demand. It could be like a radio talk show, one host sharing his or her learning, or a host interviewing a guest.

Whatever the format, podcasts can help you grow as an educator, and they can also entertain you. I have found a number of education podcasts providing meaningful professional learning, in addition to a number of entertaining noneducational podcasts prompting me to think about how I can change education for the better. Twenty-five minutes in the car? *Podcast time.* Fifteen minutes washing the dishes? *Absolutely podcast time.* Exercising or working out? *Perfect podcast time.* Folding clothes? Mowing the lawn? Cleaning bathrooms?!?! *UGH! Mandatory podcast time!*

Check out some of my favorite podcasts:

- *StartEdUp* (startedupinnovation.com/podcast) is a podcast during which Don Wettrick, a former high school innovation teacher, finds the meeting point of education, innovation, and entrepreneurship. This podcast has changed my perspective on what educators should be teaching students. Don is not afraid to ask the difficult questions educators should be asking, making this podcast a must-listen!
- *Podcast PD* (podcastpd.com) is hosted by the triumvirate of Stacey Lindes, AJ Bianco, and Chris Nesi. The show

presents a variety of topics in education, ranging from student teachers to lesson planning to running a successful Edcamp. The trio examines each topic from multiple perspectives and shares their podcast listening recommendations at the end of each episode.

- *Akimbo* (akimbo.me) is a podcast "about our culture and how we can change it," according to host, blogger, and author Seth Godin. He has examined what it takes to get into a "famous" college and even addresses what the institution of education is for in the episode titled "Stop Stealing Dreams," a personal favorite of mine.

- *Song Exploder* (songexploder.net) is a guilty pleasure for me. Each episode follows a musician or band to describe their writing process for a song. I'm fascinated by how the artists describe their creative process, and each episode teaches me a great deal about helping students with their own creative processes.

- *The Creative Classroom* (spencerauthor.com/podcast) is where John Spencer helps teachers turn their classrooms into "bastions of creativity and wonder." John shares strategies, lesson ideas, and stories in an attempt to boost innovation and creativity in the classroom. Episodes include discussions on building empathy in students, project-based learning, and engaging reluctant writers. I leave each episode with a wealth of ideas to share with colleagues about engaging students in the classroom.

For more great ideas for finding and making your own professional development, check out *The Four O'Clock Faculty: A ROGUE Guide to Revolutionizing Professional Development.*

Chapter 11

EVERY CHILD, EVERY DAY

*The best thing about being a teacher
is that it matters. The hardest thing
of teaching is that every moment
matters, every day.*

—TODD WHITAKER

What You Need to Know: Every student needs to know you care every day. While circumstances may not be perfect, or are less than ideal, each child needs to receive your best effort each and every single day. Every student deserves it.

Make a Positive Difference

If teachers have learned anything about educating children, it's this: what they do matters—every day for every child. Becoming the best teacher you can be means putting in extraordinary effort every day throughout the school year. It goes beyond just the first few days.

The positive impact that you can have on a child each day can send that same child out into the world to make his or her own positive impact.

I used to let my students know on the first day of class I wanted them to walk out of my classroom, not only as better learners, but also as better people. As nine- and ten-year-olds, the words didn't mean much to them on this first day. If I wanted those words to come true, we had to live them every day.

I had to figure out a way to get these children to truly care about each other to build community within the classroom, and then carry the kindness into the world. This is no small feat; it takes a lot of time and effort to accomplish this. There were days when I felt successful and other days when I did not. But my most meaningful contribution as a teacher was providing opportunities for students to become better people.

Every child deserves your best every day.

Every child.

Not just the easy students. Not just the ones who are academically gifted or the ones who are readily compliant.

Sometimes this is incredibly difficult. You will face times when you are dealing with a student, seeing the same behaviors over and over again, having the same conversations day in and day out, repeating the same things to a parent unwilling or unable to listen, and struggling through every consequence and intervention you are able to come up with. Through it all, the student's attitude will *not* change. And at some point, you will be ready to give up on the student and say, "I can't do this anymore. It is too difficult, and I am not strong enough. There is no way I can reach this student. I'm done."

I'm here to tell you, however, you *are* strong enough. And you have a responsibility to the child. Every child deserves your best every day. You may feel the student doesn't realize the time and effort you give, the heart and soul with which you try, and all you sacrifice in order to make a difference. They might not be recognized today or tomorrow—but they don't go unnoticed.

Show Them You Care

I once worked with a student who tested me on every level. Everything he did felt like a test of my response. He threw a chair to gauge how I would react. He walked with me in the hall, until he turned the corner where he began to run away from me, trying to escape from school. He hid under a desk and banged his head against the wall. In his weakest moments, he had zero concern for whether he hurt himself or others. He kicked me and bit me and flailed his arms at me. He yelled at me and said terrible things about my family. On many occasions, his disruptions spilled out of the classroom, involving several of my colleagues. Everyone tried to support him in reaching a calm state of being. This student also screamed at my colleagues, called some of them very unflattering names, and even hit some of them. We all realized he was not getting what he needed. In our setting, we were not able to provide the services he required. I felt we were waiting for a ticking time bomb—to explode.

But as frustrated as I was about the process to get him help taking so long, as upset as I was about his resorting to aggressive and physical behavior toward me and my colleagues, and as angry as I was at the situation, I realized, more than anything, he needed someone to care. And so I continued to greet him every morning. Asking him, "How are you today?!" served as a barometer of what kind of day we might have. We had good days and bad days—more dreadful than favorable. But the check-in each morning served to show, no matter what had transpired, I still cared about him and wanted to make sure I was attending to our relationship. Every day, I wanted to make sure he was okay.

Several months passed before we found the student a more fitting placement, which happened to be in a different school within our district. Even after he was moved to a different building, I visited him to make sure he was doing better. This wasn't an easy road, and it was by far the toughest situation I've ever faced as an educator. But I needed him to know, no matter what happened, I still cared. And on those occasions when he was having a great day, the conversations we shared brought me to a better place.

Every kid. Every day.

If there is one critical impression you take from this book, let it be this: whatever you do as an educator, you have the utmost responsibility to care about every child, and to put forth your best effort every day. It may not be smooth, it may make you uncomfortable, and you may struggle to find balance in how much you can impact a student. Even in the most difficult of situations—on the good days or the bad—every moment matters. Every interaction. Every conversation. Every relationship.

Teaching is the toughest job in the world, but it is also the most rewarding. And as you become the best educator you can be, in your own unique way, I want you to remember a few things:

Every child, whether supported or unsupported at home, needs to feel supported by you in school. You might provide nothing more than a smile, a knowing glance, or a check-in, but each student needs to know you care. The time students spend with you during the day may be the best part of their day. Recognize this and make them feel special.

Every learner needs to know you are putting forth your best effort every day. Some days may be tougher than others. You will need to make sure you are taking care of yourself first before you can take care of others. If you consistently give your best effort, it will make a difference in the eyes of your students. Even when you have a bad day, students who know you care will be able to return the favor.

Every student needs to be recognized each day. Sadly, some students go through their entire day without being acknowledged by an adult, and the attention they receive from their peers may often be negative. Serve as the bright spot in a student's day. Even when interacting with students who are not in your class, give a smile—even before Christmas!—a word of encouragement, or a high five! I often have sore hands at the end of the day from the number of high fives given. Some may prefer the fist bump, but I'm old-school.

Every scholar deserves a fresh chance every day. What happened yesterday doesn't matter. Any difficulties you or your students experienced in the past needs to be forgotten. It might be difficult to overlook an upsetting behavior, but every day is a clean break. When a child sees you give them another shot each day, your relationship will improve. She will know you care. He will trust you have his best interest at heart. Make each day a new start for every child. Each of them deserves the opportunity.

Whether you are just starting out as a teacher, have been around the profession for many years, or are somewhere in between, you have a unique opportunity every day to make a difference in the life of a child. Take advantage of this gift. Put forth your best effort each day. Yes, some days will be harder than others, but the time, effort, passion, and energy you put in each day will come back to you tenfold. If you can finish your teaching career saying, "I cared about every kid every day," you will have led a meaningful life.

SECRET SAUCE SUMMARY

- Every student deserves your best every day. Even on an "off day," you still need to put forth the effort to show students you care.

- The portion of the day students spend with you might be the best part of their days. Help them feel this way!

- Put forth your best effort every day.

- Greeting or acknowledging students every day helps them know someone cares for them. A high five, a smile, a wave, a hug—just let them know *you* are there.

- No matter what has happened with a student previously, give him or her a fresh start each day.

Planning and Reflecting

How will you show your students you care? What will you do each day?

_____

_____

_____

How will you put forth effort on the days when you don't feel like your best self? What can you do to make sure you are putting forth effort to make you and your students proud, even on your worst day?

_____

_____

_____

What steps will you need to take in order to give a student a fresh start after a particularly difficult day? What might need to happen for you and the student to move forward when there is a rough patch in your relationship?

_____

_____

_____

How can you greet or acknowledge each student each day?

_____

_____

_____

Add Your Own SECRET SAUCE Ingredients

List three actions you will take to make a difference for every student, every day.

1. _____

_____

_____

2. _____

_____

_____

3. _____

_____

_____

Chapter 12

THE RECIPE

There is no perfect spaghetti sauce.
There are only perfect spaghetti sauces.

—HOWARD MOSKOVITZ

Find Your SECRET SAUCE

Making one perfect sauce is impossible. Everyone has a different opinion on what they consider to be the perfect sauce. Some may like it sweeter. Some may like it more bitter. Some may enjoy chunky tomatoes. Some like it more like a soup. In fact, some people don't even call it sauce. I'm not even sure why, but they refer to it as *gravy*. While you cannot make the perfect sauce in education either, you *can* find *your* SECRET SAUCE—the combination of ideas, influences, resources, colleagues, strategies, and learning experiences propelling you to become the *best* educator you can be.

You've now learned about the ingredients that helped me realize my potential as an educator. You know how specific recipes can help provide meaningful and relevant learning experiences for students. First, you have to have all of the necessary ingredients. Then you have to put them together in just the right way. Then you have to let them all simmer. Your sauce may be different from the person's in the classroom next door to you, and that's okay. The beautiful part about your sauce is that you are always perfecting it. You may add some ingredients next year to improve the taste for the students you are working with at that time. You may take some of the elements away when you figure out a better way to do things. Your sauce will be constantly evolving to make you the best educator you can be.

If you are a new educator, you will need to think about how you want to approach teaching. You won't be able to walk into a classroom on day one and be the fully realized and self-actualized educator you may someday become. It will take time. You will learn. You will make mistakes. You will learn from the mistakes you make. You will need to figure out what works and doesn't work for *you*. The teacher in the classroom next door might bring a completely different brand of awesome to the table than you do, but don't be discouraged. Your "awesome" will need to be perfected over time. You will try. You will fail. You will discover. You will try again. You will reflect. You will realize. By working on your own SECRET SAUCE, you can learn to become an exceptional educator.

If you have been working with students for three years or thirty years, you should think about how you *already* approach teaching. Use the ideas presented in this book to reflect upon your own experience in the classroom. Give yourself permission to know it won't always be perfect, but you can still continue to grow as an educator. Make the learning experience better for you and your students. Use the SECRET SAUCE as a guidepost not only for how to become a more effective teacher but how to become an *exceptional* teacher. Use these ideas to rediscover the joy and passion with which you originally entered the classroom. Give yourself the gift of a fresh start.

SECRET SAUCE SUMMARY

After reading this book, you know the SECRET SAUCE is actually made by combining a number of important ingredients into your teaching strategy:

- Establishing strong relationships

- Building a positive culture

- Making a lot of mistakes

- Involving students in authentic learning opportunities where *voice* and *choice* are included

- Setting high expectations but also providing strong support

- Making connections to learn from others

- Using your time wisely

- Thinking strategically about classroom design

- Remembering "every student, every day"

Planning and Reflecting

Wherever you are in your career, what does *your* recipe look like? What ingredients will *you* include? How long will you let *your* SAUCE simmer? What other educators will *you* let help you stir your SAUCE? How will *your* SAUCE be different from those of other educators?

A Recipe for Success

Preparing Your Perfect Sauce

The time to get started is now. You know all the things I didn't know when I started. You have the secrets to help you move forward. What is your first step? How can you get started?

I would recommend starting with these five ingredients to make *your* perfect SAUCE:

1. Be positive.

- When establishing a culture in your classroom, focus on the positive. Model the behaviors you would like to see from your students.
- Make sure every student feels cared for every day.
- Even when you need to work with a student on a discipline issue, focus on the positive. Find out what's behind the behavior and support the student to move forward.
- Make sure you focus on *you* first. Practice self-care, model mindfulness for students, and make sure you take care of yourself first *so* you can take care of others too.

2. Think strategically.

- Give careful consideration to how you will set up your learning space. Give students a *voice* in what the classroom will look like and what kind of workflows are most effective for everyone.

- Determine how to most effectively use your time. Eliminate any time spent on things without value for you or your students.
- Think about how you can design learning experiences to provide students with exactly what they need.

3. Learn and keep learning

- Make connections with other passionate educators, inside and outside of your school. Learn, collaborate, and share with others to continue to grow.
- Make lots of mistakes and learn from them. It shows you are willing to try new things, to venture outside of your comfort zone, and to go beyond in order to help your students learn.
- Continue to engage in professional learning. Whether you read a book, attend a conference, meet other teachers for coffee, or listen to a podcast, find ways to grow as an educator.

4. Help students create their own learning.

- Provide authentic learning opportunities for students. Let them engage in learning experiences they are passionate about. Give students the chance to make and create content for authentic audiences.
- Establish high expectations for yourself and for students, but also create an environment providing strong support for all students to meet those expectations.
- Integrate multiple chances for *choice* within your instructional day in order to empower students to take charge of their own learning.

5. Build and strengthen relationships.

- Build relationships. Build relationships. *Build relationships!*
- Seriously, build relationships. Get to know each and every student on a deeper level. Let students know you care.
- Extend yourself and continuously strengthen relationships with parents and colleagues. Be positive and supportive. Be open and honest. Ask the question, "How can I help you?" and ask it often.

I didn't have the SECRET SAUCE when I started, and I could have been a much better educator much earlier if I had. What's great about my experience, however, is that others can learn from it, too. As everyone grows as an educator, the profession and craft will continue to improve.

Find your SECRET SAUCE. Share it. Continue to learn and grow *with* others. You have everything you need to be successful. You have everything you need to be an *exceptional educator*!

Go forth and go beyond to provide meaningful learning experiences for every student, every day.

Make all of us proud. Most of all, make yourself proud.

Now that you know the *secret*, seize it and become the *best* educator YOU can be!

Find exclusive chapter resources and more SECRET SAUCE information here:

fouroclockfaculty.com/secretsauce

NOTES

Jensen, Eric. *Teaching with the Brain in Mind, 2nd Ed*. (Alexandria, VA: Association for Supervision and Curriculum Development, 2005.)

ACKNOWLEDGMENTS

Thank you to all of the educators, past and present, who have helped me to find my SECRET SAUCE.

To the Elms family, who first welcomed me with open arms as a brand-new teacher: Liz T., Angela, Kyle, Katie, Holly, Jen, Liz V., and Theresa.

To Sue, who served as my mentor and taught me the greatest lesson I ever learned as a teacher: every decision I ever made has been done in the best interests of students.

To Cindy, my "helper teacher" and partner-in-crime. We made the best team, and much of what I learned about good teaching came from you.

To Darlene and Marybeth. Even though we only spent a short amount of time together, I learned so much from both of you.

To the rest of the Elms family who helped me transition from one classroom to many classrooms: Carol, Jillian, Justin, Donna, Sherri, Sharon, Tiffany, Carl, Kristie, Chris, and Nick.

To Dan, who taught me much of what I needed to know in order to be a good administrator, including his greatest lesson: to be present and visible always.

To Mike B., my cofounder in "Four Thumbs." You helped me grow into the educator I am today.

To the extended Jackson family, who helped me grow every day: Effie, Mike R., Rob A., Heather, Mike G., Lincoln, Aju, Rob R., Tina, and Mike S.

To Anthony and Karen, who gave me a chance even though I was late.

To George, who helped me realize what was possible in education.

To Bill D., Chris W., and Joy, who challenged me to be the best educator I could be.

To the rest of the Stafford Family who helped me to grow as an educator, Jenny, Kristin, Clark, Carl, Margaret, Dave, Vic, Marge, Dawn, Susan, Bill W., Lori, and Stephanie.

To Alex, who pushed and inspired me, and talked me through every step of the way.

To the TR family, who are still a part of my heart (I♥TR): Marielena, Jill, Deb, Gabby H., Manna, Lindsey, Karen, Mary, Jen, Colleen, Jess N., Kim, Alison, Jill, Sally, Megan, Marie, Brittany, Gabby M., Barry, James, Carolyn, Deb, Emma, Ashley K., Shaun, Lucia, Alma, and Beth.

To the extended Waterford family, who helped support me every day: Ashley P., Brenda, Patrick, Dan, Ryan, Candice, Idalis, Jessica, and Betty.

To those educators, near and far, who challenge me to be better every day: Jay B., the #4OCFpln, Stacey, Brian, Adam, Dave, Shelley, Dr. Mary, Beth, and Nili.

To my new YES family, thank you for helping me continue my journey!

To Trevor, who was there from the start, has stood with me each step of the way, and continues to challenge and inspire me each day!

More from

DAVE BURGESS
Consulting, Inc.

Since 2012, DBCI has been publishing books that inspire and equip educators to be their best. For more information on our DBCI titles or to purchase bulk orders for your school, district, or book study, visit **DaveBurgessconsulting.com/DBCIbooks**.

More from the *Like a PIRATE*™ Series

Teach Like a PIRATE by Dave Burgess

eXPlore Like a Pirate by Michael Matera

Learn Like a Pirate by Paul Solarz

Play Like a Pirate by Quinn Rollins

Run Like a Pirate by Adam Welcome

Lead Like a PIRATE™ Series

Lead Like a PIRATE by Shelley Burgess and Beth Houf

Balance Like a Pirate by Jessica Cabeen, Jessica Johnson, and Sarah Johnson

Lead beyond Your Title by Nili Bartley

Lead with Culture by Jay Billy

Lead with Literacy by Mandy Ellis

Leadership & School Culture

Culturize by Jimmy Casas

Escaping the School Leader's Dunk Tank by Rebecca Coda and Rick Jetter

From Teacher to Leader by Starr Sackstein

The Innovator's Mindset by George Couros

Kids Deserve It! by Todd Nesloney and Adam Welcome

Let Them Speak by Rebecca Coda and Rick Jetter

The Limitless School by Abe Hege and Adam Dovico

The Pepper Effect by Sean Gaillard

The Principled Principal by Jeffrey Zoul and Anthony McConnell

Relentless by Hamish Brewer

The Secret Solution by Todd Whitaker, Sam Miller, and Ryan Donlan

Start. Right. Now. by Todd Whitaker, Jeffrey Zoul, and Jimmy Casas

Stop. Right. Now. by Jimmy Casas and Jeffrey Zoul

They Call Me "Mr. De" by Frank DeAngelis

Unmapped Potential by Julie Hasson and Missy Lennard

Word Shift by Joy Kirr

Your School Rocks by Ryan McLane and Eric Lowe

Technology & Tools

50 Things You Can Do with Google Classroom by Alice Keeler and Libbi Miller

50 Things to Go Further with Google Classroom by Alice Keeler and Libbi Miller

140 Twitter Tips for Educators by Brad Currie, Billy Krakower, and Scott Rocco

Block Breaker by Brian Aspinall

Code Breaker by Brian Aspinall

Google Apps for Littles by Christine Pinto and Alice Keeler

Master the Media by Julie Smith

Shake Up Learning by Kasey Bell

Social LEADia by Jennifer Casa-Todd

Teaching Math with Google Apps by Alice Keeler and
  Diana Herrington

Teachingland by Amanda Fox and Mary Ellen Weeks

Teaching Methods & Materials

All 4s and 5s by Andrew Sharos

Boredom Busters by Katie Powell

The Classroom Chef by John Stevens and Matt Vaudrey

Ditch That Homework by Matt Miller and Alice Keeler

Ditch That Textbook by Matt Miller

Don't Ditch That Tech by Matt Miller, Nate Ridgway, and
  Angelia Ridgway

EDrenaline Rush by John Meehan

Educated by Design by Michael Cohen, The Tech Rabbi

The EduProtocol Field Guide by Marlena Hebern and
  Jon Corippo

The EduProtocol Field Guide: Book 2 by Marlena Hebern and
  Jon Corippo

Instant Relevance by Denis Sheeran

LAUNCH by John Spencer and A.J. Juliani

Make Learning MAGICAL by Tisha Richmond

Pure Genius by Don Wettrick

The Revolution by Darren Ellwein and Derek McCoy

Shift This! by Joy Kirr

Spark Learning by Ramsey Musallam

Sparks in the Dark by Travis Crowder and Todd Nesloney

Table Talk Math by John Stevens

The Wild Card by Hope and Wade King

The Writing on the Classroom Wall by Steve Wyborney

Inspiration, Professional Growth & Personal Development

Be REAL by Tara Martin

Be the One for Kids by Ryan Sheehy

Creatively Productive by Lisa Johnson

Educational Eye Exam by Alicia Ray

The EduNinja Mindset by Jennifer Burdis

Empower Our Girls by Lynmara Colón and Adam Welcome

The Four O'Clock Faculty by Rich Czyz

How Much Water Do We Have? by Pete and Kris Nunweiler

P Is for Pirate by Dave and Shelley Burgess

A Passion for Kindness by Tamara Letter

The Path to Serendipity by Allyson Apsey

Sanctuaries by Dan Tricarico

Shattering the Perfect Teacher Myth by Aaron Hogan

Stories from Webb by Todd Nesloney

Talk to Me by Kim Bearden

Teach Me, Teacher by Jacob Chastain

Through the Lens of Serendipity by Allyson Apsey

The Zen Teacher by Dan Tricarico

Children's Books

Beyond Us by Aaron Polansky

Dolphins in Trees by Aaron Polansky

I Want to Be a Lot by Ashley Savage

The Princes of Serendip by Allyson Apsey

Zom-Be a Design Thinker by Amanda Fox

BRING RICH TO YOUR NEXT SCHOOL OR DISTRICT PROFESSIONAL DEVELOPMENT EVENT

Rich Czyz is available for consulting opportunities, speaking engagements, presentations, professional development sessions, speeches, and keynote addresses on a wide range of relevant education topics. He specializes in the following topics:

- Getting Started as a New Teacher
- Personalized Professional Development
- Student Engagement Strategies
- Integrating Technology Across the Curriculum
- Educational Leadership
- Positive School Climate and Culture
- Student Ownership, Voice, and Choice
- Using Data to Guide Instruction

Please contact Rich via e-mail at 4oclockfaculty@gmail.com to learn more about consulting and speaking opportunities.

ABOUT THE AUTHOR

Rich Czyz started his educational career in 2003 as a fifth-grade teacher. During his time in the classroom, he forced his principal to remove all of the desks from his room in favor of tables and angered textbook fans everywhere by simply leaving the books on a shelf and not using them. As a basic skills teacher and instructional coach, Rich continued to push the boundaries, implementing new technology and finding better ways to do things. As an administrator, he first served as a curriculum supervisor, then director of curriculum, where he learned that sometimes challenging the status quo is really the only way to do things. Rich currently serves as the Proud Principal of the Yardville Elementary School in New Jersey, where he loves to show students what Wiffle Ball is all about.

Rich is the cofounder of *The Four O'Clock Faculty* blog for educators looking to improve instruction and learning for themselves and their students. Rich is also the author of *The Four O'Clock Faculty: A ROGUE Guide to Revolutionizing Professional Development*. Rich is passionate about engaging all stakeholders in meaningful and relevant learning. He is an author, blogger, and presenter.

Learn more about Rich by following him on Twitter at @RACzyz or visiting fouroclockfaculty.com.

CPSIA information can be obtained
at www.ICGtesting.com
Printed in the USA
LVHW082346140221
679314LV00037B/763